COMMON WORSHIP

Initiation Services

COMMON WORSHIP

Initiation Services

CHURCH HOUSE
PUBLISHING

Published by Church House Publishing,
Church House, Great Smith Street,
London SW1P 3NZ

Text © The Central Board of Finance of the Church of England 1997, 1998

Authorized edition first published 1998

ISBN 0 7151 3810 3

All rights reserved. No part of this publication may be reproduced in any form or by any means, electronic or mechanical, including photocopying, recording, or any information storage and retrieval system, except as stated below, without written permission which should be sought from the Copyright Manager, Central Board of Finance, Church House, Great Smith Street, London SW1P 3NZ.

Texts for local use: the arrangements which apply to local editions of services cover reproduction on a non-commercial basis both for a single occasion and for repeated use. Details are available in a booklet *A Brief Guide to Liturgical Copyright*. See also Copyright Information on page 206.

Editorial, cover and page design by AD Publishing Services
Printed in England by University Printing House, Cambridge

Contents

Authorization

The Initiation Services in this publication are authorized pursuant to Canon B 2 of the Canons of the Church of England for use from 11 April 1998 until further resolution of the General Synod of the Church of England.

NOTE

These services may be subject to minor textual adjustment in future printings in the interests of harmonization with the style of other material in *Common Worship*.

Introduction

These services are part of a new generation of liturgical provision in the Church of England called *Common Worship* and intended to serve the Church in its primary tasks of worship and mission.

They are all closely related to baptism and are influenced by an increasing rediscovery of the importance and meaning of baptism which is common to many churches. They owe their shape both to a new appreciation of the ancient practice of the Church, reflected for example in the *Book of Common Prayer*, and also to fresh thinking about the nature of baptism as expressing the identity and call of the Christian community today. An important part of the preparatory work was done by a working party drawn from the Board of Mission, the Board of Education and the Liturgical Commission which in 1995 produced a report to the House of Bishops entitled *On The Way: Towards an Integrated Approach to Christian Initiation* (CHP 1995). The thinking and recommendations of this report have significantly shaped these services.

This book contains

- This introduction, which gives some of the background thinking to the services, shows how they are structured and gives guidance on their use.
- Two groups of services:
  Holy Baptism: a single rite for both adults and children, presented in several ways to allow for use in different circumstances; the options given are not exhaustive and other legal variations are of course possible. Appendices include additional material, seasonal and responsive prayers and suggested readings.
  Baptism, Confirmation, Affirmation of Baptismal Faith and Reception into the Communion of the Church of England: a range of services recognizing that a person's spiritual journey does not always fall into one pattern.
- A more detailed commentary on the material.

Other forms of service and prayers are in preparation. These include Thanksgiving for and Blessing of a Child, prayers for pregnancy and childbirth, and material to support someone who is formally exploring the Christian faith. Forms of prayer are also planned to support adults who are preparing for baptism or to renew their baptism in confirmation or an affirmation of baptismal faith.

Approaching the services

It is important to come to these services with a fresh mind, trying to put aside the approaches which have conditioned thinking while the ASB has been in use. The authorized text needs to be seen not as intrusive legal regulation but as a guide to performance.

The canonical expectation (Canon B 21) is that baptism takes place within the course of public worship on Sunday. Within that, there are many possibilities, and these services provide structures for baptism to take place in various contexts. These might include not only the regular celebration of the Eucharist or A Service of the Word, but a significant celebration of Baptism as the main service of the day.

Understanding the dramatic flow

In a service of Baptism (or of Baptism and Confirmation) the Church proclaims what God has done for his people in Christ and offers us a way of entering that movement from darkness to light, from death to life, from being self-centred to being God-centred. This dramatic movement is at the heart of the service and needs to be brought out in the way it is presented, not just by reading out a series of texts. Sometimes the rich biblical imagery of the texts will resonate with people's experience, but the heart of the celebration of baptism – what really matters to those who may not pick up the verbal nuances – is what is done.

At the start of the service, the greeting is followed by an opportunity to express thanksgiving. The Liturgy of the Word and the sermon are an opportunity to set the story of what God has done in Christ alongside our own story – to explore both the points of convergence and of difference. The presentation of the candidates and their welcome by the congregation acknowledges a shared responsibility for their growth in faith and flows naturally into a solemn renunciation of evil and the expression of the desire to follow Christ. At this stage, the candidates are identified with the believing community and reminded of the cost of discipleship by receiving the sign of the cross, the badge of the pilgrim community.

In this pilgrim faith, the community journeys to the font. The candidates express their longing for the transforming grace of God's Holy Spirit in the Prayer over the Water, and identify with the community's profession of faith as they say the Creed together. Then, supported by the community, each candidate steps alone (or is carried) to the waters to be baptized in a lonely yet corporate embracing of Christ's dying and rising. Alone, we pass from death to life, leaving sin and self drowned in the waters, from which we rise to a new life that is Christ's and shared with all the baptized.

What is the new life like? It is a life directed and empowered by the Spirit, who overshadowed Jesus as he came up from the waters of baptism. As candidates emerge from the waters, they may be clothed – putting on Christ – and anointed as a sign of their belonging with all the baptized in the royal priesthood of God's holy people. Hearing a commission or charge to live out the baptized life, they take their place in the church as they participate in the prayers of intercession, and in the action of the eucharist.

But the life of the baptized is not only what takes place in worship. It is about living out our common life in Christ in and for the community in which we are set. At the end of the service, the newly baptized are sent out with a lighted candle, as a sign of the Church's commitment to mission: 'Shine as a light in the world to the glory of God the Father.'

Planning the service

Once the structure is clear, attention must be given to the practical questions surrounding the action. It is necessary to give careful and imaginative thought to the setting and to the use of appropriate music and symbol. The generosity and transforming character of the gospel of Jesus Christ needs to be clear in the way the service is acted out.

It is essential to read not just the authorized text, but also the surrounding material:

- **Service outline** – this gives an overview of the structure and flow of the service.
- **Notes** – these occur at the beginning of each group of services and set out the basic rules and understandings that govern them. They make clear some of the possible ways the services can be used or presented.
- **Rubrics** – these explain how the action is to be carried out and indicate when choices and options are available.
- **The words of the services themselves** – spoken material has many different functions in a liturgical rite; understanding these will affect how words are spoken and presented.
- **Appendices** – these make available additional material for particular occasions or seasons, which highlight different aspects of the rich variety of baptismal imaging in the Bible.
- **Tables** – these show how the main services can be used in particular circumstances or where combined with other authorized services. Some of these possibilities are printed out in full in this book.

Common questions and further explanation about various parts of the services are placed in the Commentary at the back of the book.

The significance of baptism for the Church

These services are influenced by older traditions reflected in the *Book of Common Prayer* as well as by continued thinking in the Church that wishes to place baptism at the heart of Christian life and mission. Three themes in particular stand out in these services.

Faith as process

The celebration of baptism should not be seen in isolation from the journey to faith in Christ. This journey is itself a process of discovery and transformation within a community. A baptism service must therefore help candidate and congregation discover each other as partners within a common adventure of faith. Within this mutual journey the service has an inner logic, a movement from welcome and renunciation through to the candidate's identification with the people of God in a common faith and in shared activities of prayer, eucharist and mission.

Those who have prepared these services have paid particular attention to a call from the Anglican Communion to reintegrate mission and sacramental practice:

> The journey into faith involves a process that includes awareness of God, recognition of God's work in Christ, entering into the Christian story through the scriptures, turning to Christ as Lord, incorporation into the body of Christ, nurture within the worshipping community, and being equipped and commissioned for ministry and mission within God's world. An adequate practice of baptism will recognize all these dimensions and will enable the church to play its full part in accompanying people in this journey.
>
> *International Anglican Liturgical Consultation Toronto 1991*

The renewal of baptismal practice is an integral part of mission and evangelism. In these services the whole Church is challenged to engage in generosity and seriousness with all those who are seeking new life in Jesus Christ.

The Liturgical Commission is currently working on supplementary forms of service that may help to support the journey of adults and children to faith in Jesus Christ within the community of the Church.

Journey, story, pattern

In the spiritual formation of a new Christian there needs to be a healthy interaction between three aspects of the Christian life: *journey, story* and *pattern.*

Journey is a major image in the narrative of scripture from the call of Abraham through to the itinerant ministry of Jesus and beyond. As an image of human life and of the passage to faith it allows both for the integration of faith and human experience and also for the necessity of change and development.

Closely related to journey is the importance in human and Christian experience of *story.* It is significant that the story of Paul's conversion is told three times in the book of Acts: Christian formation must allow an individual's story to be heard and to find its place within the unfolding story of faith as it appears in the Church and in the scriptures.

Complementary to the ideas of journey or story is the theme of *pattern* or *way.* Essential to Christian formation is the appropriation of patterns of belief, prayer and behaviour that give structure and coherence to the Christian life. This is part of what the earliest Christians recognized when they called themselves The Way. The report *On The Way* gave careful attention to how patterns of life and faith are established in the life of the Christian and the Church. These services seek to recognize that journey and pattern are integral to the Christian life and need to be reflected in any approach to Christian initiation.

Christian identity

Baptism is much more than a beginning to the Christian life. It expresses the identity which is ours in Jesus Christ and the shape of the life to which we are called. This has implications both for individuals who are baptized and also for the continuing life of Christian congregations. St Paul recalled Christians to an understanding of their baptism. Baptism is a reality whose meaning has to be discovered at each stage of a person's life, whether it is a young person appropriating the implication of his or her baptism in infancy, an adult making their baptism their own in all the complex developments of a human life, or a mother or father discovering Christ anew in the responsibilities of parenthood. One test of the liturgical celebration of baptism is whether, over time, it enables the whole Church to see itself as a baptized community, called to partake in the life of God and to share in the mission of God to the world.

HOLY
BAPTISM

Service Outline
Holy Baptism at the Eucharist

Preparation

Greeting
   Thanksgiving Prayer for a Child (appendix 1)
Introduction *
   † *Presentation of the Candidates*
Collect *

Liturgy of the Word

Readings and Psalm
Gospel Reading
Sermon

Liturgy of Baptism

† Presentation of the Candidates
Decision
Signing with the Cross
Prayer over the Water *
Profession of Faith *
Baptism
Commission

Prayers

† Prayers of Intercession *
Welcome and Peace *
   † *Prayers of Intercession ***

Liturgy of the Eucharist

Preparation of the Table
Taking of the Bread and Wine
Eucharistic Prayer
Lord's Prayer
Breaking of the Bread
Giving of the Bread and Cup
Prayer after Communion *

Sending Out

Blessing *
Giving of a Lighted Candle
Dismissal

† *indicates alternative position allowed and shown in Service Outline in italics*
* *indicates alternative texts in appendices*

Service Outline
Holy Baptism outside the Eucharist

Preparation

Greeting
   Thanksgiving Prayer for a Child (appendix 1)
Introduction *
   † *Presentation of the Candidates*
Collect *

Liturgy of the Word

Readings and Psalm
Gospel Reading
Sermon

Liturgy of Baptism

† Presentation of the Candidates
Decision
Signing with the Cross
Prayer over the Water *
Profession of Faith *
Baptism
Commission
   † *Prayers of Intercession* *
Welcome and Peace *

Prayers

† Prayers of Intercession *
Lord's Prayer

Sending Out

Blessing *
Giving of a Lighted Candle
Dismissal

† *indicates alternative position allowed and shown in Service Outline in italics*
* *indicates alternative texts in appendices*

Notes

Holy Baptism is normally administered by the parish priest in the course of public worship on Sunday 'when the most number of people come together' (Canon B 21).

1 Minister of Baptism

Where rubrics speak of 'the president', this indicates the parish priest or other minister authorized to administer Holy Baptism. When the bishop is present he normally presides over the whole service. Parts of the service not assigned to the president may be delegated to others.

2 Ordering of the Service

Pages 19-71 show how baptism is to be administered at the Eucharist, Morning or Evening Prayer, or A Service of the Word. The structure of the service, however, enables it to be used as a significant celebration on its own and there may be occasions where such a celebration of Holy Baptism forms a main Sunday act of worship.

3 Thanksgiving Prayer for a Child

This option (see Appendix 1) may be used where it is appropriate to express thanksgiving for a child to be baptized later in the service; this may be inserted as part of the Preparation. This is not intended to preclude the use of a separate service of Thanksgiving for the Birth of a Child.

4 Presentation of the Candidates

The Presentation may follow the Introduction where circumstances make this appropriate.

5 Collect, Readings and Other Variable Texts

The collect and readings for the Sunday should normally be used, especially on Sundays between the First Sunday of Advent and the Feast of the Presentation of Christ, and between the First Sunday of Lent and Trinity Sunday. The collects provided in the rite and its appendices may, however, be substituted on Sundays between the Presentation of Christ and the beginning of Lent and between Trinity Sunday and the beginning of Advent even when the normal Sunday readings are used. The collects and readings provided in the service or in its appendices are for use on occasions when baptism is the predominant element in the service. The basic form of the service remains constant. Within this structure seasonal material may also be used (see Appendix 2, 3 and 5). This is linked to occasions in the Christian year when its use might be particularly appropriate.

6 Godparents and Sponsors

The term 'godparent' is used for those asked to present children for baptism and to continue to support them. The term 'sponsor' is used for those who agree to support in the journey of faith candidates (of any age) for baptism, confirmation or affirmation of baptismal faith. It is not necessary that a candidate have the same person as godparent and sponsor. When children who are old enough to speak are baptized, such children, at the discretion of the parish priest, also answer the questions at the Decision with parents and godparents.

7 Hymns and Silence

If occasion requires, hymns may be sung and silence may be kept at points other than those which are indicated.

8 Corporate Responses

When members of a family are baptized at the same time, the questions at the Decision may be answered in the form 'We reject ...'

9 Profession of Faith

The whole congregation joins in the Apostles' Creed at the Profession of Faith or makes the responses in the Alternative Profession of Faith (Appendix 7).

10 Use of Oil

Where it has been agreed that oil will be used, pure olive oil, reflecting the practice of athletes preparing for a contest, may be used for the Signing with the Cross. Oil mixed with fragrant spices (traditionally called chrism), expressing the blessings of the messianic era and the richness of the Holy Spirit, may be used to accompany the prayer after the baptism. It is appropriate that the oil should have been consecrated by the bishop.

11 Signing with the Cross

At the Signing with the Cross, after the president or other minister has made the sign using the words provided, parents, godparents and sponsors may also be invited to make the sign of the cross. It is sufficient if the people join in and say their part once only, when all the candidates have been signed. The possibility of signing with the cross at the prayer after the baptism is provided for, but if this is done it should be accompanied by the text provided at that point in the rite, not the text provided for the Signing with the Cross after the Decision. If signing takes place after the baptism, it must follow the administration of water as a separate action.

12 Administration of Water

A threefold administration of water (whether by dipping or pouring) is a very ancient practice of the Church and is commended as testifying to the faith of the Trinity in which candidates are baptized. Nevertheless, a single administration is also lawful and valid. The use of a substantial amount of water is desirable; water must at least flow on the skin of the candidate. The president may delegate the act of baptism to another lawful minister.

13 Conditional Baptism

If it is not certain whether a person has already been baptized with water in the name of the Father, and of the Son, and of the Holy Spirit, then the usual service of baptism is used, but the form of words at the baptism shall be

> N, if you have not already been baptized, I baptize you in the name of the Father, and of the Son, and of the Holy Spirit. **Amen.**

14 Clothing

Provision is made for clothing after the baptism. This may be a practical necessity where dipping is the mode of baptism employed; the text provided draws on ancient tradition, linking practical necessity and scriptural imagery.

15 Prayers of Intercession

General intercession should normally be part of the service. Such prayers draw the newly baptized into the praying church of which they are now a part. It may be appropriate for the newly baptized to introduce sections of these prayers. Prayers in responsive form are provided; one of the forms of prayer in Appendix 3 and 4 may be used. The Prayers may be used after the Welcome and Peace.

16 Giving of a Lighted Candle

The Paschal candle or another large candle is made ready so that it may be lit at the Decision. Individual candles may be lit from it and given to candidates as part of the Sending Out. The giving of lighted candles may take place at an earlier stage in the service, after the administration of baptism.

Holy Baptism

Preparation

At the entry of the ministers a hymn may be sung.

GREETING

The president says

> The grace of our Lord Jesus Christ,
> the love of God
> and the fellowship of the Holy Spirit
> be with you all
> **and also with you.**

Words of welcome or introduction may be said.

The president may use the prayer of thanksgiving in Appendix 1.

INTRODUCTION

The president uses these or other words
(seasonal forms are provided in Appendix 2)

> Our Lord Jesus Christ has told us
> that to enter the kingdom of heaven
> we must be born again of water and the Spirit,
> and has given us baptism as the sign and seal of
>   this new birth.
> Here we are washed by the Holy Spirit and made clean.
> Here we are clothed with Christ,
> dying to sin that we may live his risen life.
> As children of God, we have a new dignity
> and God calls us to fullness of life.

Gloria in Excelsis may be used.

COLLECT

The president introduces a period of silent prayer with the words
Let us pray *or a more specific bidding.*

*Either the collect of the day, or this collect is said
(seasonal forms are provided in Appendix 2)*

> Heavenly Father,
> by the power of your Holy Spirit
> you give to your faithful people new life in the
>   water of baptism.
> Guide and strengthen us by the same Spirit,
> that we who are born again may serve you in faith
>   and love,
> and grow into the full stature of your Son, Jesus Christ,
> who is alive and reigns with you in the unity of
>   the Holy Spirit
> now and for ever. **Amen.**

Liturgy of the Word

READINGS

*The readings of the day are normally used on Sundays and principal
festivals. For other occasions a Table of Readings is provided in
Appendix 5.*

*Either one or two readings from scripture precede the gospel reading.
At the end of each the reader may say*

> This is the word of the Lord.
> **Thanks be to God.**

*The psalm or canticle follows the first reading; other hymns and songs
may be used between the readings.*

GOSPEL READING

An acclamation may herald the gospel reading.

When the gospel is announced the reader says

> Hear the gospel of our Lord Jesus Christ according to *N.*
> **Glory to you, O Lord.**

At the end
>This is the gospel of the Lord.
>**Praise to you, O Christ.**

SERMON

Liturgy of Baptism

PRESENTATION OF THE CANDIDATES

The candidates are presented to the congregation. Where appropriate, they are presented by their godparents or sponsors.

The president asks those candidates for baptism who are able to answer for themselves

>Do you wish to be baptized?
>**I do.**

Testimony by the candidate(s) may follow.

The president addresses the whole congregation

>Faith is the gift of God to his people.
>In baptism the Lord is adding to our number those whom
>   he is calling.
>People of God, will you welcome *these children/candidates*
>   and uphold *them* in *their* new life in Christ?
>**With the help of God, we will.**

At the baptism of children, the president then says to the parents and godparents

>Parents and godparents, the Church receives *these children*
>with joy. Today we are trusting God for *their* growth in
>faith. Will you pray for *them,* draw *them* by your example
>into the community of faith and walk with *them* in the
>way of Christ?
>**With the help of God, we will.**

In baptism *these children* begin *their* journey in faith. You speak for *them* today. Will you care for *them*, and help *them* to take *their* place within the life and worship of Christ's Church?
With the help of God, we will.

DECISION

A large candle may be lit. The president addresses the candidates directly, or through their parents, godparents and sponsors

In baptism, God calls us out of darkness into his
    marvellous light.
To follow Christ means dying to sin and rising to
    new life with him.
Therefore I ask:

Do you reject the devil and all rebellion against God?
I reject them.
Do you renounce the deceit and corruption of evil?
I renounce them.
Do you repent of the sins that separate us from
    God and neighbour?
I repent of them.

Do you turn to Christ as Saviour?
I turn to Christ.
Do you submit to Christ as Lord?
I submit to Christ.
Do you come to Christ, the way, the truth and the life?
I come to Christ.

SIGNING WITH THE CROSS

The president or another minister makes the sign of the cross on the forehead of each candidate, saying

Christ claims you for his own.
Receive the sign of his cross.

The president may invite parents, godparents and sponsors to sign the candidates with the cross. When all the candidates have been signed, the president says

> Do not be ashamed to confess the faith of Christ crucified.
> **Fight valiantly as a disciple of Christ**
> **against sin, the world and the devil,**
> **and remain faithful to Christ to the end of your life.**
>
> May almighty God deliver you from the
>   powers of darkness,
> restore in you the image of his glory,
> and lead you in the light and obedience of Christ. **Amen.**

PRAYER OVER THE WATER

The ministers and candidates gather at the baptismal font. A canticle, psalm, hymn or litany may be used (see suggestions in Appendix 5 and 6).

The president stands before the water of baptism and says (optional seasonal and responsive forms are provided in Appendix 2 and 3)

> Praise God who made heaven and earth,
> **who keeps his promise for ever.**
>
> Let us give thanks to the Lord our God.
> **It is right to give him thanks and praise.**
>
> We thank you, almighty God, for the gift of water
> to sustain, refresh and cleanse all life.
> Over water the Holy Spirit moved in the
>   beginning of creation.
> Through water you led the children of Israel
> from slavery in Egypt to freedom in the promised land.
> In water your Son Jesus received the baptism of John
> and was anointed by the Holy Spirit as the Messiah,
>   the Christ,
> to lead us from the death of sin to newness of life.

We thank you, Father, for the water of baptism.
In it we are buried with Christ in his death.
By it we share in his resurrection.
Through it we are reborn by the Holy Spirit.
Therefore, in joyful obedience to your Son,
we baptize into his fellowship those who come
    to him in faith.

Now sanctify this water that, by the power of
    your Holy Spirit,
they may be cleansed from sin and born again.
Renewed in your image, may they walk by the
    light of faith
and continue for ever in the risen life of Jesus Christ
    our Lord;
to whom with you and the Holy Spirit
be all honour and glory, now and for ever. **Amen.**

PROFESSION OF FAITH

The president addresses the congregation

Brothers and sisters, I ask you to profess
together with *these candidates*
the faith of the Church.

Do you believe and trust in God the Father?
I believe in God, the Father almighty,
creator of heaven and earth.

Do you believe and trust in his Son Jesus Christ?
I believe in Jesus Christ, his only Son, our Lord,
who was conceived by the Holy Spirit,
born of the Virgin Mary,
suffered under Pontius Pilate,
was crucified, died, and was buried;
he descended to the dead.
On the third day he rose again;
he ascended into heaven,
he is seated at the right hand of the Father,
and he will come to judge the living
    and the dead.

Do you believe and trust in the Holy Spirit?
I believe in the Holy Spirit,
the holy catholic Church,
the communion of saints,
the forgiveness of sins,
the resurrection of the body,
and the life everlasting. Amen.

Where there are strong pastoral reasons the Alternative Profession of Faith in Appendix 7 may be used.

BAPTISM

If the candidate(s) can answer for themselves, the president may say to each one
   N, is this your faith?

Each candidate answers in their own words, or
   This is my faith.

The president or another minister dips each candidate in water, or pours water on them, saying
   N, I baptize you
   in the name of the Father,
   and of the Son,
   and of the Holy Spirit. **Amen.**

If the newly baptized are clothed with a white robe, a hymn or song may be used, and then a minister may say
   You have been clothed with Christ.
   As many as are baptized into Christ have put
      on Christ.

If those who have been baptized were not signed with the cross immediately after the Decision, the president signs each one now.

The president says

> May God, who has received you by baptism
>   into his Church,
> pour upon you the riches of his grace,
> that within the company of Christ's pilgrim people
> you may daily be renewed by his anointing Spirit,
> and come to the inheritance of the saints in glory. **Amen.**

The president and those who have been baptized may return from the font.

COMMISSION

Either

Where the newly baptized are unable to answer for themselves, a minister addresses the congregation, parents and godparents

> We have brought *these children* to baptism knowing that Jesus died and rose again for *them* and trusting in the promise that God hears and answers prayer. We have prayed that in Jesus Christ *they* will know the forgiveness of *their* sins and the new life of the Spirit.
>
> As *they* grow up, *they* will need the help and encouragement of the Christian community, so that *they* may learn to know God in public worship and private prayer, follow Jesus Christ in the life of faith, serve *their* neighbour after the example of Christ, and in due course come to confirmation.
>
> As part of the Church of Christ, we all have a duty to support *them* by prayer, example and teaching. As *their* parents and godparents, you have the prime responsibility for guiding and helping *them* in *their* early years. This is a demanding task for which you will need the help and grace of God. Therefore let us now pray for grace in guiding *these children* in the way of faith.

Faithful and loving God,
bless those who care for *these children*
and grant them your gifts of love, wisdom and faith.
Pour upon them your healing and reconciling love,
and protect their home from all evil.
Fill them with the light of your presence
and establish them in the joy of your kingdom,
through Jesus Christ our Lord. **Amen.**

God of grace and life,
in your love you have given us
a place among your people;
keep us faithful to our baptism,
and prepare us for that glorious day
when the whole creation will be made perfect
in your Son our Saviour Jesus Christ. **Amen.**

If the newly baptized are old enough to understand, these words may be added

N and N,
today God has touched you with his love
and given you a place among his people.
God promises to be with you
in joy and in sorrow,
to be your guide in life,
and to bring you safely to heaven.
In baptism God invites you on a life-long journey.
Together with all God's people
you must explore the way of Jesus
and grow in friendship with God,
in love for his people,
and in serving others.
With us you will listen to the word of God
and receive the gifts of God.

or

To the newly baptized who are able to answer for themselves, a minister says

> Those who are baptized are called to worship
>   and serve God.
>
> Will you continue in the apostles' teaching
>   and fellowship,
> in the breaking of bread, and in the prayers?
> **With the help of God, I will.**
>
> Will you persevere in resisting evil,
> and, whenever you fall into sin, repent and return
>   to the Lord?
> **With the help of God, I will.**
>
> Will you proclaim by word and example
> the good news of God in Christ?
> **With the help of God, I will.**
>
> Will you seek and serve Christ in all people,
> loving your neighbour as yourself?
> **With the help of God, I will.**
>
> Will you acknowledge Christ's authority over
>   human society,
> by prayer for the world and its leaders,
> by defending the weak, and by seeking peace and justice?
> **With the help of God, I will.**
>
> May Christ dwell in your heart(s) through faith,
> that you may be rooted and grounded in love
> and bring forth the fruit of the Spirit. **Amen.**

PRAYERS OF INTERCESSION

Either here or after the Welcome and Peace intercessions are led by the president or others. These or other suitable words may be used. Other forms are provided in Appendix 2 and 4. The intercession may conclude with a collect.

> As a royal priesthood, let us pray to the Father
> through Christ who ever lives to intercede for us.

Reveal your kingdom among the nations;
may peace abound and justice flourish.
Especially for ...
Your name be hallowed.
Your kingdom come.

Send down upon us the gift of the Spirit
and renew your Church with power from on high.
Especially for ...
Your name be hallowed.
Your kingdom come.

Deliver the oppressed, strengthen the weak,
heal and restore your creation.
Especially for ...
Your name be hallowed.
Your kingdom come.

Rejoicing in the fellowship of the Church on earth,
we join our prayers with all the saints in glory.
Your name be hallowed.
Your kingdom come.

WELCOME AND PEACE

There is one Lord, one faith, one baptism:
N and N, by one Spirit we are all baptized into one body.
We welcome you into the fellowship of faith;
we are children of the same heavenly Father;
we welcome you.

The congregation may greet the newly baptized.

*The president introduces the Peace in these or other suitable words
(seasonal forms are provided in Appendix 2)*

We are all one in Christ Jesus.
We belong to him through faith,
heirs of the promise of the Spirit of peace.

The peace of the Lord be always with you.
And also with you.

A minister may say

Let us offer one another a sign of peace.

All may exchange a sign of peace.

If the Liturgy of the Eucharist does not follow immediately, the service continues with suitable prayers, ending with the Lord's Prayer and the Sending Out.

Liturgy of the Eucharist

The Eucharist continues with

PREPARATION OF THE TABLE

TAKING OF THE BREAD AND WINE

EUCHARISTIC PRAYER

This proper preface may be used

And now we give you thanks
because by water and the Holy Spirit
you have made us a holy people in Jesus Christ our Lord;
you raise us to new life in him
and renew in us the image of your glory.

LORD'S PRAYER

BREAKING OF THE BREAD

GIVING OF THE BREAD AND WINE

PRAYER AFTER COMMUNION

Either the authorized post communion prayer of the day or the
following is used (optional seasonal forms are provided in Appendix 2)

Eternal God, our beginning and our end,
preserve in your people the new life of baptism;
as Christ receives us on earth,
so may he guide us through the trials of this world
and enfold us in the joy of heaven,
where you live and reign,
one God for ever and ever. **Amen.**

Sending Out

BLESSING

The president may use a seasonal blessing (Appendix 2), or another
suitable blessing, or

The God of all grace,
who called you to his eternal glory in Christ Jesus,
establish, strengthen and settle you in the faith;
and the blessing of God almighty,
the Father, the Son and the Holy Spirit,
be upon you and remain with you always. **Amen.**

GIVING OF A LIGHTED CANDLE

The president or another person may give each of the newly baptized
a lighted candle. These may be lit from the candle used at the
Decision.

When all the newly baptized have received a candle, the president
says

God has delivered us from the dominion of darkness
and has given us a place with the saints in light.

You have received the light of Christ;
walk in this light all the days of your life.
Shine as a light in the world
to the glory of God the Father.

DISMISSAL

Go in the light and peace of Christ.
Thanks be to God.

From Easter Day to Pentecost **Alleluia Alleluia** *may be added to both the versicle and the response.*

Baptism outside the Eucharist

Preparation

At the entry of the ministers a hymn may be sung.

GREETING

The president says

> The grace of our Lord Jesus Christ,
> the love of God
> and the fellowship of the Holy Spirit
> be with you all
> **and also with you.**

Words of welcome or introduction may be said.

The president may use the prayer of thanksgiving in Appendix 1.

INTRODUCTION

*The president uses these or other words
(seasonal forms are provided in Appendix 2)*

> Our Lord Jesus Christ has told us
> that to enter the kingdom of heaven
> we must be born again of water and the Spirit,
> and has given us baptism as the sign and seal
>   of this new birth.
> Here we are washed by the Holy Spirit and made clean.
> Here we are clothed with Christ,
> dying to sin that we may live his risen life.
> As children of God, we have a new dignity
> and God calls us to fullness of life.

Gloria in Excelsis may be used.

COLLECT

The president introduces a period of silent prayer with the words
Let us pray *or a more specific bidding.*

Either the collect of the day, or this collect is said
(seasonal forms are provided in Appendix 2)

> Heavenly Father,
> by the power of your Holy Spirit
> you give to your faithful people new life in the
> water of baptism.
> Guide and strengthen us by the same Spirit,
> that we who are born again may serve you
> in faith and love,
> and grow into the full stature of your Son, Jesus Christ,
> who is alive and reigns with you in the unity of
> the Holy Spirit
> now and for ever. **Amen.**

Liturgy of the Word

READINGS

The readings of the day are normally used on Sundays and principal
festivals. For other occasions a Table of Readings is provided in
Appendix 5.

Either one or two readings from scripture precede the gospel reading.
At the end of each the reader may say

> This is the word of the Lord.
> **Thanks be to God.**

The psalm or canticle follows the first reading; other hymns and songs
may be used between the readings.

GOSPEL READING

An acclamation may herald the gospel reading.

When the gospel is announced the reader says

Hear the gospel of our Lord Jesus Christ according to *N*.
Glory to you, O Lord.

At the end

This is the gospel of the Lord.
Praise to you, O Christ.

SERMON

Liturgy of Baptism

PRESENTATION OF THE CANDIDATES

The candidates are presented to the congregation. Where appropriate, they are presented by their godparents or sponsors.

The president asks those candidates for baptism who are able to answer for themselves

Do you wish to be baptized?
I do.

Testimony by the candidate(s) may follow.

The president addresses the whole congregation

Faith is the gift of God to his people.
In baptism the Lord is adding to our number those whom
   he is calling.
People of God, will you welcome *these children/candidates*
   and uphold *them* in *their* new life in Christ?
With the help of God, we will.

At the baptism of children, the president then says to the parents and godparents

Parents and godparents, the Church receives *these children* with joy. Today we are trusting God for *their* growth in faith. Will you pray for *them*, draw *them* by your example into the community of faith and walk with *them* in the way of Christ?
With the help of God, we will.

In baptism *these children* begin *their* journey in faith. You speak for *them* today. Will you care for *them*, and help *them* to take *their* place within the life and worship of Christ's Church?
With the help of God, we will.

DECISION

A large candle may be lit. The president addresses the candidates directly, or through their parents, godparents and sponsors.

In baptism, God calls us out of darkness into his
    marvellous light.
To follow Christ means dying to sin and rising to
    new life with him.
Therefore I ask:

Do you reject the devil and all rebellion against God?
I reject them.
Do you renounce the deceit and corruption of evil?
I renounce them.
Do you repent of the sins that separate us from
    God and neighbour?
I repent of them.

Do you turn to Christ as Saviour?
I turn to Christ.
Do you submit to Christ as Lord?
I submit to Christ.
Do you come to Christ, the way, the truth and the life?
I come to Christ.

SIGNING WITH THE CROSS

The president or another minister makes the sign of the cross on the forehead of each candidate, saying

Christ claims you for his own.
Receive the sign of his cross.

The president may invite parents, godparents and sponsors to sign the candidates with the cross. When all the candidates have been signed, the president says

Do not be ashamed to confess the faith of Christ crucified.
Fight valiantly as a disciple of Christ
against sin, the world and the devil,
and remain faithful to Christ to the end of your life.

May almighty God deliver you from the
powers of darkness,
restore in you the image of his glory,
and lead you in the light and obedience of Christ. **Amen.**

PRAYER OVER THE WATER

The ministers and candidates gather at the baptismal font. A canticle, psalm, hymn or litany may be used (texts are suggested in Appendix 5 and 6).

The president stands before the water of baptism and says (optional seasonal and responsive forms are provided in Appendix 2 and 3)

Praise God who made heaven and earth,
who keeps his promise for ever.

Let us give thanks to the Lord our God.
It is right to give him thanks and praise.

We thank you, almighty God, for the gift of water
to sustain, refresh and cleanse all life.
Over water the Holy Spirit moved in the
    beginning of creation.
Through water you led the children of Israel
from slavery in Egypt to freedom in the promised land.
In water your Son Jesus received the baptism of John
and was anointed by the Holy Spirit as the Messiah,
    the Christ,
to lead us from the death of sin to newness of life.

We thank you, Father, for the water of baptism.
In it we are buried with Christ in his death.
By it we share in his resurrection.
Through it we are reborn by the Holy Spirit.
Therefore, in joyful obedience to your Son,
we baptize into his fellowship those who come
    to him in faith.

Now sanctify this water that, by the power of
    your Holy Spirit,
they may be cleansed from sin and born again.
Renewed in your image, may they walk by the
    light of faith
and continue for ever in the risen life of Jesus Christ
    our Lord;
to whom with you and the Holy Spirit
be all honour and glory, now and for ever. **Amen.**

PROFESSION OF FAITH

The president addresses the congregation

Brothers and sisters, I ask you to profess
together with *these candidates*
the faith of the Church.

Do you believe and trust in God the Father?
**I believe in God, the Father almighty,
creator of heaven and earth.**

Do you believe and trust in his Son Jesus Christ?
I believe in Jesus Christ, his only Son, our Lord,
who was conceived by the Holy Spirit,
born of the Virgin Mary,
suffered under Pontius Pilate,
was crucified, died, and was buried;
he descended to the dead.
On the third day he rose again;
he ascended into heaven,
he is seated at the right hand of the Father,
and he will come to judge the living
    and the dead.

Do you believe and trust in the Holy Spirit?
I believe in the Holy Spirit,
the holy catholic Church,
the communion of saints,
the forgiveness of sins,
the resurrection of the body,
and the life everlasting. Amen.

Where there are strong pastoral reasons the Alternative Profession of
Faith in Appendix 7 may be used.

BAPTISM

If the candidate(s) can answer for themselves, the president
may say to each one
    N, is this your faith?

Each candidate answers in their own words, or
    This is my faith.

The president or another minister dips each candidate in water, or
pours water on them, saying
    N, I baptize you
    in the name of the Father,
    and of the Son,
    and of the Holy Spirit. **Amen.**

If the newly baptized are clothed with a white robe, a hymn or song may be used, and then a minister may say

> You have been clothed with Christ.
> As many as are baptized into Christ have put
>   on Christ.

If those who have been baptized were not signed with the cross immediately after the Decision, the president signs each one now.

The president says

> May God, who has received you by baptism
>   into his Church,
> pour upon you the riches of his grace,
> that within the company of Christ's pilgrim people
> you may daily be renewed by his anointing Spirit,
> and come to the inheritance of the saints in glory. **Amen.**

The president and those who have been baptized may return from the font.

COMMISSION

Either

Where the newly baptized are unable to answer for themselves, a minister addresses the congregation, parents and godparents

> We have brought *these children* to baptism knowing that Jesus died and rose again for *them* and trusting in the promise that God hears and answers prayer. We have prayed that in Jesus Christ *they* will know the forgiveness of *their* sins and the new life of the Spirit.

> As *they* grow up, *they* will need the help and encouragement of the Christian community, so that *they* may learn to know God in public worship and private prayer, follow Jesus Christ in the life of faith, serve *their* neighbour after the example of Christ, and in due course come to confirmation.

As part of the Church of Christ, we all have a duty to support *them* by prayer, example and teaching. As *their* parents and godparents, you have the prime responsibility for guiding and helping *them* in *their* early years. This is a demanding task for which you will need the help and grace of God. Therefore let us now pray for grace in guiding *these children* in the way of faith.

One or more of the following prayers may be used

Faithful and loving God,
bless those who care for *these children*
and grant them your gifts of love, wisdom and faith.
Pour upon them your healing and reconciling love,
and protect their home from all evil.
Fill them with the light of your presence
and establish them in the joy of your kingdom,
through Jesus Christ our Lord. **Amen.**

God of grace and life,
in your love you have given us
a place among your people;
keep us faithful to our baptism,
and prepare us for that glorious day
when the whole creation will be made perfect
in your Son our Saviour Jesus Christ. **Amen.**

If the newly baptized are old enough to understand, these words may be added

N and N,
today God has touched you with his love
and given you a place among his people.
God promises to be with you
in joy and in sorrow,
to be your guide in life,
and to bring you safely to heaven.

In baptism God invites you on a life-long journey.
Together with all God's people
you must explore the way of Jesus
and grow in friendship with God,
in love for his people,
and in serving others.
With us you will listen to the word of God
and receive the gifts of God.

or

*To the newly baptized who are able to answer for themselves, a
minister says*

Those who are baptized are called to worship
    and serve God.

Will you continue in the apostles' teaching
    and fellowship,
in the breaking of bread, and in the prayers?
With the help of God, I will.

Will you persevere in resisting evil,
and, whenever you fall into sin, repent and return
    to the Lord?
With the help of God, I will.

Will you proclaim by word and example
the good news of God in Christ?
With the help of God, I will.

Will you seek and serve Christ in all people,
loving your neighbour as yourself?
With the help of God, I will.

Will you acknowledge Christ's authority over
    human society,
by prayer for the world and its leaders,
by defending the weak, and by seeking peace and justice?
With the help of God, I will.

May Christ dwell in your heart(s) through faith,
that you may be rooted and grounded in love
and bring forth the fruit of the Spirit. **Amen.**

WELCOME AND PEACE

There is one Lord, one faith, one baptism:
N and N, by one Spirit we are all baptized into one body.
We welcome you into the fellowship of faith;
we are children of the same heavenly Father;
we welcome you.

The congregation may greet the newly baptized.

The president introduces the Peace in these or other suitable words
(seasonal forms are provided in Appendix 2)

We are all one in Christ Jesus.
We belong to him through faith,
heirs of the promise of the Spirit of peace.

The peace of the Lord be always with you.
And also with you.

A minister may say
Let us offer one another a sign of peace.
All may exchange a sign of peace.

Prayers

PRAYERS OF INTERCESSION

Intercessions are led by the president or others. These or other suitable
words may be used. Other forms are provided in Appendix 2 and 4.
The intercession concludes with the Lord's Prayer.

As a royal priesthood, let us pray to the Father
through Christ who ever lives to intercede for us.

Reveal your kingdom among the nations;
may peace abound and justice flourish.
Especially for ...
Your name be hallowed.
Your kingdom come.

Send down upon us the gift of the Spirit
and renew your Church with power from on high.

Especially for ...
Your name be hallowed.
Your kingdom come.

Deliver the oppressed, strengthen the weak,
heal and restore your creation.
Especially for ...
Your name be hallowed.
Your kingdom come.

Rejoicing in the fellowship of the Church on earth,
we join our prayers with all the saints in glory.
Your name be hallowed.
Your kingdom come.

LORD'S PRAYER

Sending Out

BLESSING

The president may use a seasonal blessing (Appendix 2), or another suitable blessing, or

The God of all grace,
who called you to his eternal glory in Christ Jesus,
establish, strengthen and settle you in the faith;
and the blessing of God almighty,
the Father, the Son and the Holy Spirit,
be upon you and remain with you always. **Amen.**

GIVING OF A LIGHTED CANDLE

The president or another person may give each of the newly baptized a lighted candle. These may be lit from the candle used at the Decision.

When all the newly baptized have received a candle, the president says

> God has delivered us from the dominion of darkness
> and has given us a place with the saints in light.

> You have received the light of Christ;
> walk in this light all the days of your life.
> **Shine as a light in the world**
> **to the glory of God the Father.**

DISMISSAL

> Go in the light and peace of Christ.
> **Thanks be to God.**

From Easter Day to Pentecost Alleluia Alleluia *may be added to both the versicle and the response.*

Baptism of Children at the Eucharist

The service for *Holy Baptism* provides for baptism in the context of the Eucharist. The following notes aim to highlight the implication of this for the baptism of children at a parish's regular Sunday Eucharist.

1 The opening of the service should include an appropriate introduction and may include a prayer of thanksgiving for the child (Appendix 1).

2 The Prayers of Penitence and the Nicene Creed are omitted.

3 The Presentation of the Candidates for Baptism takes place after the sermon. Alternatively it may form part of the opening section of the service; before the Gloria or Kyries (where these are used). If the presentation is used in this earlier position, it must precede the Collect.

4 Baptism takes place after the sermon.

5 An interrogatory version of the Apostles' Creed is provided in the text, to be said by the whole congregation. The Apostles' Creed is the normal baptismal creed in the Western tradition. A shorter Profession of Faith can be found in Appendix 7.

6 The first form of the Commission is to be used at the baptism of children.

7 A brief form of the Prayers of Intercession is provided. Longer seasonal forms are to be found in Appendix 2. The Prayers may be placed before or after the Welcome. If the prayers precede the Welcome and Peace, the Liturgy of the Eucharist then continues in the usual way with the Preparation of the Table and the Taking of the Bread and Wine.

8 A lighted candle is presented to the newly baptized as part of the conclusion of the service. It may be appropriate to invite the parents and godparents to the front at this point. The candle is lit from the Paschal candle (or other large candle) previously lit at the Decision.

The following table indicates how the service for *Holy Baptism* is to be used with the services indicated.

ORDER OF BAPTISM	ASB 1980 RITE A	ASB 1980 RITE B	BCP
[Thanksgiving] Introduction	After the Greeting *[omit Prayers of Penitence]*	After the Greeting *[omit Commandments and Summary of the Law]*	After the Sermon
	Omit Nicene Creed	Omit Nicene Creed	Omit Nicene Creed
Presentation	After the Greeting or Sermon	After the Greeting or Sermon	After the Introduction
Baptism	After the Sermon	After the Sermon	After the Presentation
Prayers of Intercession	At the Intercessions *[omit Prayers of Penitence]*	At the Intercessions *[omit Prayers of Penitence]*	Use Prayers of Intercession from *Holy Baptism* in place of Prayer for Church Militant
Welcome and Peace	At the Peace	At the Peace	Use the Welcome after the Commission
Prayer after Communion	After the Giving of Bread and Wine	After the Giving of Bread and Wine	Do not use
Giving of a Lighted Candle	Between the Blessing and Dismissal	Between the Blessing and Dismissal	After the Blessing

Baptism of Children at the Eucharist

Preparation

At the entry of the ministers a hymn may be sung.

GREETING

The president says

> The grace of our Lord Jesus Christ,
> the love of God
> and the fellowship of the Holy Spirit
> be with you all
> **and also with you.**

Words of welcome or introduction may be said.

The president may use the prayer of thanksgiving in Appendix 1.

INTRODUCTION

The president uses these or other words
(seasonal forms are provided in Appendix 2)

> Our Lord Jesus Christ has told us
> that to enter the kingdom of heaven
> we must be born again of water and the Spirit,
> and has given us baptism as the sign and seal of
>   this new birth.
> Here we are washed by the Holy Spirit and made clean.
> Here we are clothed with Christ,
> dying to sin that we may live his risen life.
> As children of God, we have a new dignity
> and God calls us to fullness of life.

The Presentation of the Candidates may take place either here or after the Sermon.

Gloria in Excelsis may be used.

COLLECT

The president introduces a period of silent prayer with the words
Let us pray *or a more specific bidding.*

Either the collect of the day, or this collect is said
(seasonal forms are provided in Appendix 2)

> Heavenly Father,
> by the power of your Holy Spirit
> you give to your faithful people new life in the
>   water of baptism.
> Guide and strengthen us by the same Spirit,
> that we who are born again may serve you in
>   faith and love,
> and grow into the full stature of your Son, Jesus Christ,
> who is alive and reigns with you in the unity of
>   the Holy Spirit
> now and for ever. **Amen.**

Liturgy of the Word

READINGS

The readings of the day are normally used on Sundays and principal
festivals. For other occasions a Table of Readings is provided in
Appendix 5.

Either one or two readings from scripture precede the gospel reading.
At the end of each the reader may say

> This is the word of the Lord.
> **Thanks be to God.**

The psalm or canticle follows the first reading; other hymns and songs
may be used between the readings.

GOSPEL READING

An acclamation may herald the gospel reading.

Hear the gospel of our Lord Jesus Christ according to *N*.
Glory to you, O Lord.

At the end

This is the gospel of the Lord.
Praise to you, O Christ.

SERMON

Liturgy of Baptism

PRESENTATION OF THE CANDIDATES

The candidates are presented to the congregation. Where appropriate, they are presented by their godparents or sponsors.

The president addresses the whole congregation

Faith is the gift of God to his people.
In baptism the Lord is adding to our number those whom he is calling.
People of God, will you welcome *these children/candidates* and uphold *them* in *their* new life in Christ?
With the help of God, we will.

The president then says to the parents and godparents

Parents and godparents, the Church receives *these children* with joy. Today we are trusting God for *their* growth in faith. Will you pray for *them*, draw *them* by your example into the community of faith and walk with *them* in the way of Christ?
With the help of God, we will.

In baptism *these children* begin *their* journey in faith. You speak for *them* today. Will you care for *them*, and help *them* to take *their* place within the life and worship of Christ's Church?
With the help of God, we will.

DECISION

A large candle may be lit. The president addresses the candidates through their parents, godparents and sponsors

> In baptism, God calls us out of darkness into his
>   marvellous light.
> To follow Christ means dying to sin and rising to
>   new life with him.
> Therefore I ask:
>
> Do you reject the devil and all rebellion against God?
> **I reject them.**
> Do you renounce the deceit and corruption of evil?
> **I renounce them.**
> Do you repent of the sins that separate us from
>   God and neighbour?
> **I repent of them.**
>
> Do you turn to Christ as Saviour?
> **I turn to Christ.**
> Do you submit to Christ as Lord?
> **I submit to Christ.**
> Do you come to Christ, the way, the truth and the life?
> **I come to Christ.**

SIGNING WITH THE CROSS

The president or another minister makes the sign of the cross on the forehead of each candidate, saying

> Christ claims you for his own.
> Receive the sign of his cross.

The president may invite parents, godparents and sponsors to sign the candidates with the cross. When all the candidates have been signed, the president says

> Do not be ashamed to confess the faith of Christ crucified.
> **Fight valiantly as a disciple of Christ**
> **against sin, the world and the devil,**
> **and remain faithful to Christ to the end of your life.**

May almighty God deliver you from the
    powers of darkness,
restore in you the image of his glory,
and lead you in the light and obedience of Christ. **Amen.**

PRAYER OVER THE WATER

The ministers and candidates gather at the baptismal font. A canticle, psalm, hymn or litany may be used (texts are suggested in Appendix 5 and 6).

The president stands before the water of baptism and says (optional seasonal and responsive forms are provided in Appendix 2 and 3)

Praise God who made heaven and earth,
who keeps his promise for ever.

Let us give thanks to the Lord our God.
It is right to give him thanks and praise.

We thank you, almighty God, for the gift of water
to sustain, refresh and cleanse all life.
Over water the Holy Spirit moved in the
    beginning of creation.
Through water you led the children of Israel
from slavery in Egypt to freedom in the promised land.
In water your Son Jesus received the baptism of John
and was anointed by the Holy Spirit as the Messiah,
    the Christ,
to lead us from the death of sin to newness of life.

We thank you, Father, for the water of baptism.
In it we are buried with Christ in his death.
By it we share in his resurrection.
Through it we are reborn by the Holy Spirit.
Therefore, in joyful obedience to your Son,
we baptize into his fellowship those who come to
    him in faith.

Now sanctify this water that, by the power of your
    Holy Spirit,
they may be cleansed from sin and born again.
Renewed in your image, may they walk by the
    light of faith
and continue for ever in the risen life of Jesus Christ
    our Lord;
to whom with you and the Holy Spirit
be all honour and glory, now and for ever. **Amen.**

PROFESSION OF FAITH

The president addresses the congregation

Brothers and sisters, I ask you to profess
together with *these candidates*
the faith of the Church.

Do you believe and trust in God the Father?
**I believe in God, the Father almighty,
creator of heaven and earth.**

Do you believe and trust in his Son Jesus Christ?
**I believe in Jesus Christ, his only Son, our Lord,
who was conceived by the Holy Spirit,
born of the Virgin Mary,
suffered under Pontius Pilate,
was crucified, died, and was buried;
he descended to the dead.
On the third day he rose again;
he ascended into heaven,
he is seated at the right hand of the Father,
and he will come to judge the living
    and the dead.**

Do you believe and trust in the Holy Spirit?
**I believe in the Holy Spirit,
the holy catholic Church,
the communion of saints,
the forgiveness of sins,
the resurrection of the body,
and the life everlasting. Amen.**

Where there are strong pastoral reasons the Alternative Profession of Faith in Appendix 7 may be used.

BAPTISM

The president or another minister dips each candidate in water, or pours water on them, saying

> N, I baptize you
> in the name of the Father,
> and of the Son,
> and of the Holy Spirit. **Amen.**

> > *If the newly baptized are clothed with a white robe, a hymn or song may be used, and then a minister may say*
> > You have been clothed with Christ.
> > As many as are baptized into Christ have put
> >   on Christ.
> > *If those who have been baptized were not signed with the cross immediately after the Decision, the president signs each one now.*

The president says

> May God, who has received you by baptism
>   into his Church,
> pour upon you the riches of his grace,
> that within the company of Christ's pilgrim people
> you may daily be renewed by his anointing Spirit,
> and come to the inheritance of the saints in glory. **Amen.**

The president and those who have been baptized may return from the font.

COMMISSION

A minister addresses the congregation, parents and godparents

> We have brought *these children* to baptism knowing that Jesus died and rose again for *them* and trusting in the promise that God hears and answers prayer. We have prayed that in Jesus Christ *they* will know the forgiveness of *their* sins and the new life of the Spirit.

As *they* grow up, *they* will need the help and
encouragement of the Christian community, so that *they*
may learn to know God in public worship and private
prayer, follow Jesus Christ in the life of faith, serve *their*
neighbour after the example of Christ, and in due course
come to confirmation.

As part of the Church of Christ, we all have a duty to
support *them* by prayer, example and teaching. As *their*
parents and godparents, you have the prime responsibility
for guiding and helping *them* in *their* early years. This is a
demanding task for which you will need the help and
grace of God. Therefore let us now pray for grace in
guiding *these children* in the way of faith.

One or more of the following prayers may be used

Faithful and loving God,
bless those who care for *these children*
and grant them your gifts of love, wisdom and faith.
Pour upon them your healing and reconciling love,
and protect their home from all evil.
Fill them with the light of your presence
and establish them in the joy of your kingdom,
through Jesus Christ our Lord. **Amen.**

God of grace and life,
in your love you have given us
a place among your people;
keep us faithful to our baptism,
and prepare us for that glorious day
when the whole creation will be made perfect
in your Son our Saviour Jesus Christ. **Amen.**

If the newly baptized are old enough to understand, these words may be added

> N *and* N,
> today God has touched you with his love
> and given you a place among his people.
> God promises to be with you
> in joy and in sorrow,
> to be your guide in life,
> and to bring you safely to heaven.
> In baptism God invites you on a life-long journey.
> Together with all God's people
> you must explore the way of Jesus
> and grow in friendship with God,
> in love for his people,
> and in serving others.
> With us you will listen to the word of God
> and receive the gifts of God.

PRAYERS OF INTERCESSION

Either here or after the Welcome and Peace intercessions are led by the president or others. These or other suitable words may be used. Other forms are provided in Appendix 2 and 4. The intercession may conclude with a collect.

> As a royal priesthood, let us pray to the Father
> through Christ who ever lives to intercede for us.
>
> Reveal your kingdom among the nations;
> may peace abound and justice flourish.
> *Especially for ...*
> Your name be hallowed.
> **Your kingdom come.**
>
> Send down upon us the gift of the Spirit
> and renew your Church with power from on high.
> *Especially for ...*
> Your name be hallowed.
> **Your kingdom come.**

Deliver the oppressed, strengthen the weak,
heal and restore your creation.
Especially for ...
Your name be hallowed.
Your kingdom come.

Rejoicing in the fellowship of the Church on earth,
we join our prayers with all the saints in glory.
Your name be hallowed.
Your kingdom come.

WELCOME AND PEACE

There is one Lord, one faith, one baptism:
N and N, by one Spirit we are all baptized into one body.
We welcome you into the fellowship of faith;
we are children of the same heavenly Father;
we welcome you.

The congregation may greet the newly baptized.

The president introduces the Peace in these or other suitable words
(seasonal forms are provided in Appendix 2)

We are all one in Christ Jesus.
We belong to him through faith,
heirs of the promise of the Spirit of peace.

The peace of the Lord be always with you.
And also with you.

> *A minister may say*
> Let us offer one another a sign of peace.
> *All may exchange a sign of peace.*

Liturgy of the Eucharist

The Eucharist continues with

PREPARATION OF THE TABLE

TAKING OF THE BREAD AND WINE

EUCHARISTIC PRAYER

This proper preface may be used

> And now we give you thanks
> because by water and the Holy Spirit
> you have made us a holy people in Jesus Christ our Lord;
> you raise us to new life in him
> and renew in us the image of your glory.

LORD'S PRAYER

BREAKING OF THE BREAD

GIVING OF THE BREAD AND WINE

PRAYER AFTER COMMUNION

Either the authorized post communion prayer of the day or the
following is used (optional seasonal forms are provided in Appendix 2)

> Eternal God, our beginning and our end,
> preserve in your people the new life of baptism;
> as Christ receives us on earth,
> so may he guide us through the trials of this world
> and enfold us in the joy of heaven,
> where you live and reign,
> one God for ever and ever. **Amen.**

Sending Out

BLESSING

The president may use a seasonal blessing (Appendix 2), or another suitable blessing, or

> The God of all grace,
> who called you to his eternal glory in Christ Jesus,
> establish, strengthen and settle you in the faith;
> and the blessing of God almighty,
> the Father, the Son and the Holy Spirit,
> be upon you and remain with you always. **Amen.**

GIVING OF A LIGHTED CANDLE

The president or another person may give each of the newly baptized a lighted candle. These may be lit from the candle used at the Decision.

When all the newly baptized have received a candle, the president says

> God has delivered us from the dominion of darkness
> and has given us a place with the saints in light.

> You have received the light of Christ;
> walk in this light all the days of your life.
> **Shine as a light in the world**
> **to the glory of God the Father.**

DISMISSAL

> Go in the light and peace of Christ.
> **Thanks be to God.**

From Easter Day to Pentecost **Alleluia Alleluia** *may be added to both the versicle and the response.*

Baptism of Children at A Service of the Word

Any minister may preside over A Service of the Word, the Prayers and the Commission. The minister of baptism, who is the parish priest or other minister authorized to administer Holy Baptism, must preside over the Liturgy of Baptism.

Headings on this page refer to the service for *Holy Baptism*.

Where alternative forms are provided in the service for *Holy Baptism*, they may be used with A Service of the Word.

1 The Prayers of Penitence are not used.

2 The Creed or Affirmation of Faith is replaced by the Profession of Faith.

3 The Introduction, Thanksgiving Prayer for a Child, and Presentation of the Candidates may be used as part of the Preparation or after the Liturgy of the Word.

4 The following sections are used after the Liturgy of the Word:

> PRESENTATION OF THE CANDIDATES [if not used earlier]
> DECISION
> SIGNING WITH THE CROSS
> PRAYER OVER THE WATER
> PROFESSION OF FAITH
> BAPTISM
> COMMISSION
> WELCOME AND PEACE

Alternatively the Peace may be used later in the service or omitted.

5 The Prayers of Intercession may be used before or after the Welcome or later in the service.

6 The Giving of a Lighted Candle takes place at the conclusion of the service. Alternatively it may take place after the administration of baptism.

The headings in the service which follows are primarily those from A Service of the Word, incorporating appropriate sections from the service for *Holy Baptism*.

Baptism of Children at A Service of the Word

Preparation

GREETING

The minister welcomes the people with a liturgical Greeting.

Venite, Kyries, Gloria, a hymn, song or set of responses may be used.

The minister may use the prayer of thanksgiving in Appendix 1.

INTRODUCTION

*The minister may use these or other words
(seasonal forms are provided in Appendix 2)*

> Our Lord Jesus Christ has told us
> that to enter the kingdom of heaven
> we must be born again of water and the Spirit,
> and has given us baptism as the sign and seal of this
> new birth.
> Here we are washed by the Holy Spirit and
> made clean.
> Here we are clothed with Christ,
> dying to sin that we may live his risen life.
> As children of God, we have a new dignity
> and God calls us to fullness of life.

COLLECT

*The collect is said either here or as part of the Intercessions and
Thanksgivings.*

Either the collect of the day, or this collect is said
(seasonal forms are provided in Appendix 2)

> Heavenly Father,
> by the power of your Holy Spirit
> you give to your faithful people new life in the
>   water of baptism.
> Guide and strengthen us by the same Spirit,
> that we who are born again may serve you in faith
>   and love,
> and grow into the full stature of your Son, Jesus Christ,
> who is alive and reigns with you in the unity of
>   the Holy Spirit
> now and for ever. **Amen.**

The Presentation of the Candidates may take place either here or after
the Sermon.

Liturgy of the Word

This includes

READINGS *(or a reading) from Holy Scripture*

PSALM, *or, if occasion demands, a scriptural song*

SERMON

Liturgy of Baptism

PRESENTATION OF THE CANDIDATES

The candidates are presented to the congregation. Where appropriate,
they are presented by their godparents or sponsors.

The minister of baptism addresses the whole congregation

Faith is the gift of God to his people.
In baptism the Lord is adding to our number those whom
he is calling.
People of God, will you welcome *these children/candidates*
and uphold *them* in *their* new life in Christ?
With the help of God, we will.

The minister of baptism then says to the parents and godparents

Parents and godparents, the Church receives *these children*
with joy. Today we are trusting God for *their* growth in
faith. Will you pray for *them,* draw *them* by your example
into the community of faith and walk with *them* in the
way of Christ?
With the help of God, we will.

In baptism *these children* begin *their* journey in faith. You
speak for *them* today. Will you care for *them,* and help
them to take *their* place within the life and worship of
Christ's Church?
With the help of God, we will.

DECISION

A large candle may be lit. The minister of baptism addresses the
candidates through their parents, godparents and sponsors

In baptism, God calls us out of darkness into his
marvellous light.
To follow Christ means dying to sin and rising to
new life with him.
Therefore I ask:

Do you reject the devil and all rebellion against God?
I reject them.
Do you renounce the deceit and corruption of evil?
I renounce them.
Do you repent of the sins that separate us from
God and neighbour?
I repent of them.

Do you turn to Christ as Saviour?
I turn to Christ.
Do you submit to Christ as Lord?
I submit to Christ.
Do you come to Christ, the way, the truth and the life?
I come to Christ.

SIGNING WITH THE CROSS

The minister of baptism or another minister makes the sign of the cross on the forehead of each candidate, saying

Christ claims you for his own.
Receive the sign of his cross.

The minister of baptism may invite parents, godparents and sponsors to sign the candidates with the cross. When all the candidates have been signed, the minister of baptism says

Do not be ashamed to confess the faith of Christ crucified.
Fight valiantly as a disciple of Christ
against sin, the world and the devil,
and remain faithful to Christ to the end of your life.

May almighty God deliver you from the
    powers of darkness,
restore in you the image of his glory,
and lead you in the light and obedience of Christ. **Amen.**

PRAYER OVER THE WATER

The ministers and candidates gather at the baptismal font. A canticle, psalm, hymn or litany may be used (texts are suggested in Appendix 5 and 6).

The minister of baptism stands before the water of baptism and says (optional seasonal and responsive forms are provided in Appendix 2 and 3)

Praise God who made heaven and earth,
who keeps his promise for ever.

Let us give thanks to the Lord our God.
It is right to give him thanks and praise.

We thank you, almighty God, for the gift of water
to sustain, refresh and cleanse all life.
Over water the Holy Spirit moved in the beginning
of creation.
Through water you led the children of Israel
from slavery in Egypt to freedom in the promised land.
In water your Son Jesus received the baptism of John
and was anointed by the Holy Spirit as the Messiah,
the Christ,
to lead us from the death of sin to newness of life.

We thank you, Father, for the water of baptism.
In it we are buried with Christ in his death.
By it we share in his resurrection.
Through it we are reborn by the Holy Spirit.
Therefore, in joyful obedience to your Son,
we baptize into his fellowship those who come
to him in faith.

Now sanctify this water that, by the power of your
Holy Spirit,
they may be cleansed from sin and born again.
Renewed in your image, may they walk by the
light of faith
and continue for ever in the risen life of Jesus Christ
our Lord;
to whom with you and the Holy Spirit
be all honour and glory, now and for ever. **Amen.**

PROFESSION OF FAITH

The minister of baptism addresses the congregation

Brothers and sisters, I ask you to profess
together with *these candidates*
the faith of the Church.

Do you believe and trust in God the Father?
I believe in God, the Father almighty,
creator of heaven and earth.

Do you believe and trust in his Son Jesus Christ?
I believe in Jesus Christ, his only Son, our Lord,

who was conceived by the Holy Spirit,
born of the Virgin Mary,
suffered under Pontius Pilate,
was crucified, died, and was buried;
he descended to the dead.
On the third day he rose again;
he ascended into heaven,
he is seated at the right hand of the Father,
and he will come to judge the living
 and the dead.

Do you believe and trust in the Holy Spirit?
I believe in the Holy Spirit,
the holy catholic Church,
the communion of saints,
the forgiveness of sins,
the resurrection of the body,
and the life everlasting. Amen.

*Where there are strong pastoral reasons the Alternative Profession of
Faith in Appendix 7 may be used.*

BAPTISM

*The minister of baptism or another minister dips each candidate in
water, or pours water on them, saying*

N, I baptize you
in the name of the Father,
and of the Son,
and of the Holy Spirit. **Amen.**

> *If the newly baptized are clothed with a white robe, a hymn
> or song may be used, and then a minister may say*
>
> You have been clothed with Christ.
> As many as are baptized into Christ have put
> on Christ.
>
> *If those who have been baptized were not signed with the
> cross immediately after the Decision, the minister of baptism
> signs each one now.*

The minister of baptism says

> May God, who has received you by baptism
>   into his Church,
> pour upon you the riches of his grace,
> that within the company of Christ's pilgrim people
> you may daily be renewed by his anointing Spirit,
> and come to the inheritance of the saints in glory. **Amen.**

The minister of baptism and those who have been baptized may return from the font.

The Giving of a Lighted Candle may take place here, if not at the end of the service.

COMMISSION

A minister addresses the congregation, parents and godparents

> We have brought *these children* to baptism knowing that Jesus died and rose again for *them* and trusting in the promise that God hears and answers prayer. We have prayed that in Jesus Christ *they* will know the forgiveness of *their* sins and the new life of the Spirit.
>
> As *they* grow up, *they* will need the help and encouragement of the Christian community, so that *they* may learn to know God in public worship and private prayer, follow Jesus Christ in the life of faith, serve *their* neighbour after the example of Christ, and in due course come to confirmation.
>
> As part of the Church of Christ, we all have a duty to support *them* by prayer, example and teaching. As *their* parents and godparents, you have the prime responsibility for guiding and helping *them* in *their* early years. This is a demanding task for which you will need the help and grace of God. Therefore let us now pray for grace in guiding *these children* in the way of faith.

Faithful and loving God,
bless those who care for *these children*
and grant them your gifts of love, wisdom and faith.
Pour upon them your healing and reconciling love,
and protect their home from all evil.
Fill them with the light of your presence
and establish them in the joy of your kingdom,
through Jesus Christ our Lord. **Amen.**

God of grace and life,
in your love you have given us
a place among your people;
keep us faithful to our baptism,
and prepare us for that glorious day
when the whole creation will be made perfect
in your Son our Saviour Jesus Christ. **Amen.**

If the newly baptized are old enough to understand, these words may be added

N and N,
today God has touched you with his love
and given you a place among his people.
God promises to be with you
in joy and in sorrow,
to be your guide in life,
and to bring you safely to heaven.
In baptism God invites you on a life-long journey.
Together with all God's people
you must explore the way of Jesus
and grow in friendship with God,
in love for his people,
and in serving others.
With us you will listen to the word of God
and receive the gifts of God.

Prayers

These include

INTERCESSIONS AND THANKSGIVINGS

These may be taken from the service for Holy Baptism.

LORD'S PRAYER

WELCOME AND PEACE

There is one Lord, one faith, one baptism:
N and N, by one Spirit we are all baptized into one body.
We welcome you into the fellowship of faith;
we are children of the same heavenly Father;
we welcome you.

The congregation may greet the newly baptized.

*The minister introduces the Peace in these or other suitable words
(seasonal forms are provided in Appendix 2)*

We are all one in Christ Jesus.
We belong to him through faith,
heirs of the promise of the Spirit of peace.

The peace of the Lord be always with you.
And also with you.

A minister may say
Let us offer one another a sign of peace.
All may exchange a sign of peace.

Sending Out

The service concludes with a liturgical Ending.

BLESSING

GIVING OF A LIGHTED CANDLE

The minister or another person may give each of the newly baptized a lighted candle. These may be lit from the candle used at the Decision.

When all the newly baptized have received a candle, the minister says

God has delivered us from the dominion of darkness
and has given us a place with the saints in light.

You have received the light of Christ;
walk in this light all the days of your life.
**Shine as a light in the world
to the glory of God the Father.**

DISMISSAL

Go in the light and peace of Christ.
Thanks be to God.

From Easter Day to Pentecost **Alleluia Alleluia** *may be added to both the versicle and the response.*

Baptism of Children at Morning or Evening Prayer

When appropriate, the service of Morning Prayer or Evening Prayer may be abbreviated. The Prayers of Penitence may be omitted, and the Creed is omitted, being replaced by one of the interrogatory forms provided in the service for *Holy Baptism*.

The service follows this order (the headings refer to the parts of the service for *Holy Baptism*). Alternative positions are indicated in italics.

The introduction to the service may include:

THANKSGIVING PRAYER FOR A CHILD
INTRODUCTION
PRESENTATION OF THE CANDIDATES

Morning or Evening Prayer to the end of the second reading.

Then follow:

PRESENTATION OF THE CANDIDATES [if not used earlier]
DECISION
SIGNING WITH THE CROSS
PRAYER OVER THE WATER
PROFESSION OF FAITH
BAPTISM
COMMISSION
WELCOME
PEACE

Morning or Evening Prayer from the canticle after the second reading to the end of the service, omitting the Apostles' Creed. At the prayers, appropriate intercessions from the service for *Holy Baptism* may be used.

The service concludes with:

BLESSING
GIVING OF A LIGHTED CANDLE
DISMISSAL

Thanksgiving Prayer for a Child

This prayer may be used after the Greeting.

> We rejoice today with the *family* of *N and N*
> as they thank God for the gift of life
> and bring their *children* for baptism.
>
> God our creator,
> we thank you for the wonder of new life
> and for the mystery of human love.
> We give thanks for all whose support and skill
> surround and sustain the beginning of life.
> As Jesus knew love and discipline within a human family,
> may *these children* grow in strength and wisdom.
> As Mary knew the joys and pains of motherhood,
> give *these parents* your sustaining grace and love;
> through Jesus Christ our Lord. **Amen.**

The service continues with the Introduction and Collect.

Appendix 2

Seasonal Material

This section contains seasonal texts to supplement those printed in the service for Holy Baptism.

The material in each set of seasonal texts comprises: Introduction, Collect, Prayer over the Water, words at the Peace, Prayers of Intercession, Prayer after Communion and Blessing. Responsive forms of the Prayer over the Water are given in Appendix 3.

Sets of readings are provided in Appendix 5, grouped under four headings: General; Epiphany/Baptism of Christ/Trinity; Easter/Pentecost; All Saints.

The headings (Epiphany/Baptism of Christ/Trinity, Easter/Pentecost and All Saints) indicate the seasonal emphases of the material.

Epiphany/Baptism of Christ/Trinity

INTRODUCTION

At our Lord's baptism in the river Jordan
God showed himself to all who have eyes to see
　　and ears to hear.
The Father spoke from heaven, the Spirit descended
　　as a dove
and Jesus was anointed with power from on high.
Here is the door of faith,
through which we enter the kingdom of heaven.
As children of God, we are adopted as his sons
　　and daughters,
and called to proclaim the wonders of him
who called us out of darkness into his marvellous light.

COLLECT

Lord of all time and eternity,
you opened heaven's gate and revealed yourself as Father
by the voice that called Jesus your beloved Son,
baptizing him, in the power of the Spirit:
reveal yourself to us now, to claim us as your children,
and so complete the heavenly work of our rebirth
in the waters of the new creation;
through Jesus Christ your Son our Lord who is alive and
    reigns with you,
in the unity of the Holy Spirit,
one God, now and for ever. **Amen.**

PRAYER OVER THE WATER

Praise God who made heaven and earth,
who keeps his promise for ever.

Let us give thanks to the Lord our God.
It is right to give him thanks and praise.

Father, we give you thanks and praise
for your gift of water in creation;
for your Spirit, sweeping over the waters,
bringing light and life;
for your Son Jesus Christ our Lord,
baptized in the river Jordan.

We bless you for your new creation,
brought to birth by water and the Spirit,
and for your grace bestowed upon us your children,
washing away our sins.

May your holy and life-giving Spirit
move upon these waters.
Restore through them the beauty of your creation,
and bring those who are baptized
to new birth in the family of your Church.

Drown sin in the waters of judgement,
anoint your children with power from on high,
and make them one with Christ
in the freedom of your kingdom.
For all might, majesty, dominion and power are yours,
now and for ever.
Alleluia. Amen.

PEACE

If anyone is in Christ, there is a new creation.
The old has passed away; the new has come.

PRAYERS OF INTERCESSION

God of glory,
whose radiance shines from the face of Christ,
give your children such assurance of your mercy
and such knowledge of your grace,
that, believing all you promise,
and receiving all you give,
they may be transformed ever more closely
by your Spirit into the image of Jesus, your Son.

Father of life,
make known your glory.

God of light,
whose life shines beyond all things,
give us and all your Church
the will to follow Christ
and to bear his peace,
that the light of Christ
may bring confidence to the world,
and faithfulness to all who look to you in hope.

Father of life,
make known your glory.

God of power,
whose word gives life to heaven and earth,
pour your abundant gifts on all your creation,
that the blind may see, the fallen may be raised,
and your people find tongues to confess
your promises of a broken world made new.

Father of life,
make known your glory.

If the Eucharist does not follow, the prayers end with the Lord's Prayer.

In baptism God declares that we are his children,
whom he loves;
so let us pray:
Our Father ...

PRAYER AFTER COMMUNION

God of glory,
you inspire us with the breath of life
which brought to birth a new world in Christ.
May we who are reborn in him
be transformed by the renewal of our lives,
that the light of your new creation
may flood the world with your abundant grace;
through Christ our Lord. **Amen.**

BLESSING

God, who in his Christ gives us a spring of water
welling up to eternal life,
perfect in you the image of his glory;
and the blessing ...

Easter/Pentecost

INTRODUCTION

God raised Jesus Christ from the dead
and sent the Holy Spirit to recall the whole
   world to himself.
In baptism we die to sin and rise to newness of
   life in Christ.
Here we find rebirth in the Spirit,
and set our minds on his heavenly gifts.
As children of God, we are continually created anew,
as we walk the path of faith,
and feed on the forgiveness of his healing grace.

COLLECT

Father of our Lord Jesus Christ,
from whose wounded side flowed life for the world:
raise your people from sin and death
and build them as living stones
into the spiritual temple of your Church;
through Jesus Christ your Son our Lord,
who lives and reigns with you in the unity of
   the Holy Spirit,
one God, world without end. **Amen.**

PRAYER OVER THE WATER

Praise God who made heaven and earth,
who keeps his promise for ever.

Let us give thanks to the Lord our God.
It is right to give him thanks and praise.

Almighty God, whose Son Jesus Christ
was baptized in the river Jordan:
we thank you for the gift of water
to cleanse us and revive us.

We thank you that through the waters of the Red Sea
you led your people out of slavery to freedom in the
    promised land.

We thank you that through the deep waters of death
you brought your Son, and raised him to life in triumph.

Bless this water, that your servants who are washed in it
may be made one with Christ in his death and in
    his resurrection,
to be cleansed and delivered from all sin.

Send your Holy Spirit upon them,
bring them to new birth in the household of faith,
and raise them with Christ to full and eternal life;
for all might, majesty, authority, and power are yours,
now and for ever. **Amen.**

PEACE

The risen Christ came and stood among his disciples
and said 'Peace be with you'.
Then were they glad when they saw the Lord.

or

God has made us one in Christ.
He has set his seal upon us, and as a pledge of
    what is to come
has given us the Spirit to dwell in our hearts.

PRAYERS OF INTERCESSION

Father, we thank you that by baptism you have raised
these your children with Christ to new life in the Spirit.
Guide and protect them with your grace,
that they may follow you all their days
and grow in knowledge and love of you.

Father, by the victory of your Son,
give light to the world.

May Christ who conquered sin and death
keep his whole Church faithful to his gospel.
Help us always to hold fast to truth
and to walk in the way of life.

Father, by the victory of your Son,
give light to the world.

May the Holy Spirit fill the hearts and minds of all nations
to unite the world in peace and love.
By your healing power restore all that is broken
and unite us with you, our God and Father.

Father, by the victory of your Son,
give light to the world.

If the Eucharist does not follow, the prayers end with the Lord's Prayer.

Raised again with Christ in the power of the Spirit, we say:
Our Father ...

PRAYER AFTER COMMUNION

Author of life divine,
in the resurrection of your Son, you set before us
the mystery of his triumph over sin and death;
may all who are washed in the waters of rebirth
rise to newness of life
and find the promised presence of your abundant grace;
through Jesus Christ our Lord. **Amen.**

BLESSING

God the Father, by whose glory Christ was raised
  from the dead,
strengthen you by his life-giving Spirit
to walk with him in the paths of righteousness and peace;
and the blessing ...

All Saints

INTRODUCTION

In baptism, God calls us to be his friends
and to make us holy in his Son Jesus Christ.
On this journey of faith we have no abiding city,
for we have the promise of the heavenly Jerusalem,
where the whole creation is brought to a new birth in the
    Holy Spirit.
Here we are united in the company of all the faithful,
and we look for the coming of the eternal kingdom.
As children of God, we look through this passing age
for the signs of the dawn of everlasting glory.

COLLECT

Almighty Father,
you have made us heirs through hope of your
    everlasting kingdom,
and in the waters of baptism you have promised
a measure of grace overflowing to all eternity.
Take our sins and guilt away,
and so inflame us with the life of your Spirit
that we may know your favour and goodness towards us,
and walk in newness of life, both now and for ever;
through Jesus Christ your Son our Lord,
who is alive and reigns with you,
in the unity of the Holy Spirit,
one God, now and for ever. **Amen.**

PRAYER OVER THE WATER

Praise God who made heaven and earth,
who keeps his promise for ever.

Let us give thanks to the Lord our God.
It is right to give him thanks and praise.

Lord of the heavens,
we bless your name for all your servants
who have been a sign of your grace through the ages.

You delivered Noah from the waters of destruction;
you divided the waters of the sea,
and by the hand of Moses
you led your people from slavery
into the promised land.

You made a new covenant in the blood of your Son,
that all who confess your name
may, by the Holy Spirit,
enter the covenant of grace,
receive a pledge of the kingdom of heaven,
and share in the divine nature.

Fill these waters, we pray, with the power of that
    same Spirit,
that all who enter them may be reborn,
and rise from the grave to new life in Christ.

As the apostles and prophets, the confessors and martyrs,
faithfully served you in their generation,
may we be built into an eternal dwelling for you,
through Jesus Christ our Lord,
to whom with you and the Holy Spirit
be honour and glory, now and for ever. **Amen.**

PEACE

May the God of peace make you perfect and holy,
that you may be kept safe and blameless in spirit, soul,
    and body,
for the coming of our Lord Jesus Christ.

or

We are fellow-citizens with the saints
and of the household of God
through Christ our Lord,
who came and preached peace to those who were far off
and those who were near.

PRAYERS OF INTERCESSION

Heavenly Father,
receive into the arms of your mercy
all who have been baptized
and make them your own for ever;
that, having tasted of your goodness,
they may ever hunger for your continuing presence
in their walk of faith.

Your kingdom come.
Your will be done.

Stir up within your Church the zeal that inspires
your saints in every generation.
Give us a due sense of your grace,
and the strength to do your will.
You measure us by our needs;
may we never measure you by our impatience.

Your kingdom come.
Your will be done.

Surrounded by so great a company of witnesses,
may we honour your blessings
in all the ages that have gone before,
and live in joyful expectation
of your promises in the ages yet to come.

Your kingdom come.
Your will be done.

If the Eucharist does not follow, the prayers end with the Lord's Prayer.

Remember us Lord in your heavenly kingdom
as we your children unite our prayers with your Son:
Our Father ...

PRAYER AFTER COMMUNION

Lord, in the vision of your heavenly kingdom
you reveal among us the promise of your glory;
may that glory be ours
as we claim our citizenship in the kingdom
where you are alive and reign, one God, for ever and ever.
Amen.

BLESSING

May God, who kindled the fire of his love in the hearts of
the saints,
give you joy in their fellowship,
and strengthen you to follow them in the way of holiness;
and the blessing ...

Responsive Forms of the Prayer over the Water

General

The refrain **Lord of life, renew your creation** *may be said or sung. The first phrase (italicized) may be said or sung by a deacon or other minister.*

Praise God who made heaven and earth,
who keeps his promise for ever.

Let us give thanks to the Lord our God.
It is right to give him thanks and praise.

We thank you, almighty God, for the gift of water
to sustain, refresh and cleanse all life.
Over water the Holy Spirit moved in the beginning
    of creation.
Through water you led the children of Israel
from slavery in Egypt to freedom in the promised land.
In water your Son Jesus received the baptism of John
and was anointed by the Holy Spirit as the Messiah,
    the Christ,
to lead us from the death of sin to newness of life.
Lord of life,
renew your creation.

We thank you, Father, for the water of baptism.
In it we are buried with Christ in his death.
By it we share in his resurrection.
Through it we are reborn by the Holy Spirit.
Therefore, in joyful obedience to your Son,
we baptize into his fellowship those who come to
    him in faith.
Lord of life,
renew your creation.

Now sanctify this water that, by the power of
　　your Holy Spirit,
they may be cleansed from sin and born again.
Renewed in your image, may they walk by the
　　light of faith
and continue for ever in the risen life of Jesus Christ
　　our Lord;
to whom with you and the Holy Spirit
be all honour and glory, now and for ever. **Amen.**
Lord of life,
renew your creation.

Epiphany/Baptism of Christ/Trinity

Praise God who made heaven and earth,
who keeps his promise for ever.

Let us give thanks to the Lord our God.
It is right to give him thanks and praise.

Father, for your gift of water in creation,
we give you thanks and praise.

For your Spirit, sweeping over the waters,
bringing light and life,
we give you thanks and praise.

For your Son Jesus Christ our Lord,
baptized in the river Jordan,
we give you thanks and praise.

For your new creation,
brought to birth by water and the Spirit,
we give you thanks and praise.

For your grace bestowed upon us your children,
washing away our sins,
we give you thanks and praise.

Father, accept our sacrifice of praise;
may your holy and life-giving Spirit
move upon these waters.
Lord, receive our prayer.

Restore through them the beauty of your creation,
and bring those who are baptized
to new birth in the family of your Church.
Lord, receive our prayer.

Drown sin in the waters of judgement,
anoint your children with power from on high,
and make them one with Christ
in the freedom of your kingdom.
Lord, receive our prayer.

For all might, majesty and dominion are yours,
now and for ever.
Alleluia. Amen.

Easter/Pentecost

*The refrain **Saving God, give us life** may be said or sung. The first
phrase (italicized) may be said or sung by a deacon or other minister.*

Praise God who made heaven and earth,
who keeps his promise for ever.

Let us give thanks to the Lord our God.
It is right to give him thanks and praise.

Almighty God, whose Son Jesus Christ
was baptized in the river Jordan,
we thank you for the gift of water
to cleanse us and revive us.
Saving God,
give us life.

We thank you that through the waters of the Red Sea
you led your people out of slavery
to freedom in the promised land.
Saving God,
give us life.

We thank you that through the deep waters of death
you brought your Son,
and raised him to life in triumph.
Saving God,
give us life.

Bless this water, that your servants who are washed in it
may be made one with Christ in his death and in
   his resurrection,
to be cleansed and delivered from all sin.
Saving God,
give us life.

Send your Holy Spirit upon them,
bring them to new birth in the household of faith,
and raise them with Christ to full and eternal life;
for all might, majesty, authority and power are yours,
now and for ever. **Amen.**
Saving God,
give us life.

All Saints

The refrain **Hope of the Saints, make known your glory** *may be
said or sung. The first phrase (italicized) may be said or sung by a
deacon or other minister.*

Praise God who made heaven and earth,
who keeps his promise for ever.

Let us give thanks to the Lord our God.
It is right to give him thanks and praise.

Lord of the heavens,
we bless your name for all your servants
who have been a sign of your grace through the ages.
Hope of the saints,
make known your glory.

You delivered Noah from the waters of destruction;
you divided the waters of the sea,
and by the hand of Moses
you led your people from slavery
into the promised land.
Hope of the saints,
make known your glory.

You made a new covenant in the blood of your Son,
that all who confess his name
may, by the Holy Spirit,
enter the covenant of grace,
receive a pledge of the kingdom of heaven,
and share in the divine nature.
Hope of the saints,
make known your glory.

Fill these waters, we pray, with the power of that
    same Spirit,
that all who enter them may be reborn
and rise from the grave
to new life in Christ.
Hope of the saints,
make known your glory.

As the apostles and prophets, the confessors and martyrs,
faithfully served you in their generation,
may we be built into an eternal dwelling for you,
through Jesus Christ our Lord,
to whom with you and the Holy Spirit
be honour and glory, now and for ever. **Amen.**
Hope of the saints,
make known your glory.

Appendix 4

Alternative Prayers of Intercession

Seasonal alternatives are provided in Appendix 2.

The prayers may be led by the president or another minister.

We thank you that you have claimed for yourself
those who have been washed in the waters of rebirth.
Uphold them in this new life,
that they may ever remain steadfast in faith,
joyful in hope, and rooted in your love.

Father of life,
make known your glory.

Pour your blessing on all your people.
May our hearts ever praise you,
and find their perfect rest in you.
Grant us the freedom of your service
and peace in doing your will.

Father of life,
make known your glory.

The whole creation is filled with the light of your grace.
Dispel the darkness of our hearts, and forgive our sins
     and negligences,
that we may come at last to the light of your glory.

Father of life,
make known your glory.

If the Eucharist does not follow, the prayers end with the Lord's Prayer.

As your children, born again in Christ, we say:
Our Father …

Appendix 5

Bible Readings and Psalms at Holy Baptism

PSALM	OLD TESTAMENT	NEW TESTAMENT	GOSPEL
1 General			
Psalm 66.5-12	Isaiah 43.1-7	Romans 5.6-11	Mark 1.1-11(9-11)
Psalm 89.21,22, 25-9	Genesis 17.1-8 (or 22.15-18)	Galatians 3.27 – 4.7	John 15.1-11
Psalm 51.1-6	2 Kings 5.1-15a	Titus 3.3-7	John 3.1-8
Psalm 46.1-7	Genesis 7.1,7-16	1 Peter 3.18-22	Matthew 28.16-20
2 Epiphany/Baptism of Christ/Trinity			
Psalm 67	Exodus 33.12-20/ Isaiah 9.2,3,6,7	2 Corinthians 3.12 – 4.6	John 1.14-18
Psalm 146.5-9	Isaiah 42.5-8	Acts 9.(1 or)10-20	Luke 3.15-17,21,22
Psalm 50.1-6	Isaiah 63.15,16; 64.1-4	1 Corinthians 10.1-4	Mark 1.1-11
3 Easter/Pentecost			
Psalm 118.19-24	Ezekiel 37.1-14	Romans 6.3-11	Matthew 28.16-20
Psalm 51.6-13	Ezekiel 36.24-28	Titus 3.3-7	John 20.19-23
Psalm 46.1-7	Ezekiel 47.1-12	Revelation 22.1-5	John 7.37-39
4 All Saints			
Psalm 98.1-4	Exodus 19.3-8	Revelation 5.6-10	Matthew 28.16-20
Psalm 63.1-6	Isaiah 44.1-5	Hebrews 11.32 – 12.2	Matthew 5.1-12 or 16
Psalm 92.10-15	Hosea 14.4-8	1 Peter 2.4-10	John 15.1-11
5 Vigil or Post-Baptismal Liturgy			
Psalm 121	Genesis 28.10-17	Hebrews 10.(12-) 19-23	Mark 10.(13-)17-27
Psalm 114	Exodus 3.(1-)7-15	Hebrews 11.24-29	Luke 9.(51-)57-62
6 Canticles in Procession to the Font			
Isaiah 12.2-6 Psalm 42.1-7 Deuteronomy 32.1-4 A Litany of the Resurrection (Appendix 6)			

A Litany of the Resurrection
which may be used in Procession to the Baptismal Font

O give thanks to the Lord, for he is gracious:
and his mercy endures for ever.

He has loved us from all eternity:
for his mercy endures for ever.

And remembered us when we were in trouble:
for his mercy endures for ever.

For us and for our salvation he came down from heaven:
for his mercy endures for ever.

He became incarnate of the Holy Spirit and the
  Virgin Mary
and was made man:
for his mercy endures for ever.

By his cross and passion he has redeemed the world:
for his mercy endures for ever.

And has washed us from our sins in his own blood:
for his mercy endures for ever.

On the third day he rose again:
for his mercy endures for ever.

And has given us the victory:
for his mercy endures for ever.

He ascended into heaven:
for his mercy endures for ever.

And opened wide for us the everlasting doors:
for his mercy endures for ever.

He is seated at the right hand of the Father:
for his mercy endures for ever.

And ever lives to make intercession for us:
for his mercy endures for ever.

**Glory to the Father, and to the Son,
and to the Holy Spirit:
as it was in the beginning, is now,
and shall be for ever. Amen.**

For the gift of his Spirit:
blessed be Christ.

For the catholic Church:
blessed be Christ.

For the means of grace:
blessed be Christ.

For the hope of glory:
blessed be Christ.

For the triumphs of his gospel:
blessed be Christ.

For the lives of his saints:
blessed be Christ.

In joy and in sorrow:
blessed be Christ.

In life and in death:
blessed be Christ.

Now and to the end of the ages:
blessed be Christ.

Appendix 7

Alternative Profession of Faith

Where there are strong pastoral reasons, the following may be used in place of the Profession of Faith in the service for Holy Baptism.

The president says

Let us affirm,
together with these who are being baptized,
our common faith in Jesus Christ.

Do you believe and trust in God the Father,
source of all being and life,
the one for whom we exist?
I believe and trust in him.

Do you believe and trust in God the Son,
who took our human nature,
died for us and rose again?
I believe and trust in him.

Do you believe and trust in God the Holy Spirit,
who gives life to the people of God
and makes Christ known in the world?
I believe and trust in him.

This is the faith of the Church.
This is our faith.
We believe and trust in one God,
Father, Son and Holy Spirit.

Emergency Baptism

Notes

1 In an emergency, a lay person may be the minister of baptism, and should subsequently inform those who have the pastoral responsibility for the person so baptized.

2 Parents are responsible for requesting emergency baptism for an infant. They should be assured that questions of ultimate salvation or of the provision of a Christian funeral for an infant who dies do not depend upon whether or not the child has been baptized.

3 Before baptizing, the minister should ask the name of the person to be baptized. When, through the absence of parents or for some other reason, there is uncertainty as to the name of the person, the baptism can be properly administered without a name (so long as the identity of the person baptized can be duly recorded).

Form for Emergency Baptism

The following form is sufficient.

The minister pours water on the person to be baptized, saying

> I baptize you in the name of the Father, and of the Son, and of the Holy Spirit. **Amen.**

The minister may then say the Lord's Prayer and the Grace or a blessing.

If it is appropriate, some of the following may also be used.

> ### BEFORE THE BAPTISM
>
> Jesus says: I have come that you may have life
> and have it in all its fullness.   *John 10.10*
>
> All that the Father gives me will come to me;
> and whoever comes to me I will not turn away.
>   *John 6.37*

The Lord is near to the broken hearted,
and saves the crushed in spirit.   *Psalm 34.18*

Heavenly Father,
grant that by your Holy Spirit
this child may be born again
and know your love in the new creation
given us in Jesus Christ our Lord. **Amen.**

at the Signing with the Cross

N, may Christ protect and defend you.
Receive the sign of his cross.

Prayer over the Water

Heavenly Father,
bless this water,
that whoever is washed in it
may be made one with Christ
in the fellowship of your Church,
and be brought through every tribulation
to share the risen life
that is ours in Jesus Christ our Lord. **Amen.**

AFTER THE BAPTISM

Our Father ...

Eternal God, our beginning and our end,
preserve in your people the new life of baptism;
as Christ receives us on earth,
so may he guide us through the trials of this world,
and enfold us in the joy of heaven,
where you live and reign,
one God for ever and ever. **Amen.**

The grace of our Lord Jesus Christ,
the love of God,
and the fellowship of the Holy Spirit
    be with us all. **Amen.**

or

> May God almighty,
> the Father, the Son and the Holy Spirit,
> bless and keep you this day and for ever more. **Amen.**

Service in Church

Notes

1 If the person lives, they shall afterwards come to church, or be brought to church, and the service for *Holy Baptism* followed, except that the Signing with the Cross, the Prayer over the Water and the Baptism are omitted.

2 It may be appropriate to use the form of thanksgiving in Appendix 1.

3 At the Presentation the president says

> We welcome *N*, who has been baptized and now comes to take his/her place in the company of God's people.

4 Oil mixed with fragrant spices (traditionally called chrism), expressing the blessings of the messianic era and the richness of the Holy Spirit, may be used to accompany the prayer after the baptism. It is appropriate that the oil should have been consecrated by the bishop.

THE EUCHARIST
with
BAPTISM
and
CONFIRMATION
together with
AFFIRMATION OF BAPTISMAL FAITH
and
RECEPTION INTO THE COMMUNION OF THE CHURCH OF ENGLAND

Service Outline

Preparation

Greeting
    Gloria in Excelsis
Collect

Liturgy of the Word

Readings and Psalm
Gospel Reading
Sermon

Liturgy of Initiation

Presentation of the Candidates
Decision
Signing with the Cross
Prayer over the Water
Profession of Faith
Baptism
    Declarations
Confirmation
    Affirmation of Baptismal Faith
    Reception into the Communion of the Church of England
Commission
Prayers of Intercession
Welcome and Peace

Liturgy of the Eucharist

Preparation of the Table
Taking of the Bread and Wine
Eucharistic Prayer
Lord's Prayer
Breaking of the Bread
Giving of the Bread and Wine
Prayer after Communion

Sending Out

Blessing
    Giving of a Lighted Candle
Dismissal

Notes

1 Ordering of the Service

The service is presided over by the bishop and the parts reserved to the bishop are indicated. All other parts may be delegated. This may include delegating the administration of the water of baptism to another lawful minister.

The ordering of the service should take into account the arrangement of the building and its furnishings and the most appropriate way of involving those present. The places where baptism and confirmation are administered should be determined after consultation between the bishop and the parish priest. Nevertheless, wherever possible all candidates should make the profession of baptismal faith (even when there are no candidates for baptism) at the place of baptism, the font.

Provision is made for the baptism of those not able to answer for themselves. When these are children baptized at the same time as their parents, it is fitting that they are baptized immediately after their own parents. When members of a family are baptized at the same time, the questions at the Decision may be answered in the form 'We reject ...'

For the ordering of the service when there are only candidates for some of the different elements in it, see the provision on pages 118-21.

2 Affirmation of Baptismal Faith

The provision for Affirmation of Baptismal Faith is intended for those who are already baptized and confirmed and who, after preparation and instruction, come to make a public act of commitment. It is not intended for use when an entire congregation renews its baptismal vows, for which separate provision is made.

3 Testimony

If candidates are to give testimony after the Presentation, it is important that this should be appropriate in length and style and not detract from the rest of the service. The bishop may, at his discretion, allow for testimony to be made at an earlier point in the service before the sermon. Testimony may be given in written form.

4 Hymns and Silence

If occasion requires, hymns may be sung and silence may be kept at points other than those which are indicated.

5 Collect, Readings and Other Variable Texts

The collects, readings and variable prayers provided in the rite and its appendices are intended for use when the service does not form the usual Sunday service. Where baptism, confirmation, affirmation and reception take place in a usual Sunday service, the collect and readings for the Sunday should normally be used, especially on Sundays between the First Sunday of Advent and the Presentation of Christ, and between the First Sunday of Lent and Trinity Sunday.

6 Use of Oil

Where it has been agreed that oil will be used, pure olive oil, reflecting the practice of athletes preparing for a contest, may be used for the Signing with the Cross. Oil mixed with fragrant spices (traditionally called chrism), expressing the blessings of the messianic era and the richness of the Holy Spirit, may be used to accompany the confirmation and/or affirmation. Use of chrism at the prayer after baptism is not appropriate if confirmation follows immediately. It is appropriate that the oil should have been consecrated by the bishop.

7 Signing with the Cross

At the Signing with the Cross, after the bishop or other minister has made the sign using the words provided, sponsors may also be invited to make the sign of the cross. It is sufficient if the people join in and say their part once only, when all the candidates have been signed. The possibility of signing with the cross at the prayer after baptism is provided for, but if this is done it should be accompanied by the text provided at that part of the service, not the text provided for the Signing with the Cross after the Decision. If signing takes place after the baptism it must follow the administration of water as a separate act.

8 Conditional Baptism

If it is not certain whether a person has already been baptized with water in the name of the Father, and of the Son, and of the Holy Spirit, then the usual service of baptism is used, but the form of words at the baptism shall be

> *N*, if you have not already been baptized, I baptize you in the name of the Father, and of the Son, and of the Holy Spirit.
> **Amen.**

9 Profession of Faith

The whole congregation joins in the Apostles' Creed at the Profession of Faith.

10 Clothing

Provision is made for clothing after the baptism. This may be a practical necessity where dipping is the mode of baptism employed; the text provided draws on ancient tradition, linking practical necessity and scriptural imagery.

11 Prayers of Intercession

The forms of prayer provided in the service for *Holy Baptism* may be used for the Prayers of Intercession.

12 The Blessing

When the bishop presides, the blessing may be preceded by the following

Our help is in the name of the Lord,
who has made heaven and earth.

Blessed be the name of the Lord,
now and for ever. Amen.

13 Giving of a Lighted Candle

The Paschal candle, or another large candle, may be lit at the Decision and individual candles may be lit from it and given to candidates, including the newly confirmed, as part of the Sending Out. The giving of lighted candles to the newly baptized may take place at an earlier stage in the rite after the administration of baptism, in which case candles are not given to the newly confirmed.

The Eucharist with Baptism and Confirmation together with Affirmation of Baptismal Faith and Reception into the Communion of the Church of England

Preparation

At the entry of the ministers, a hymn may be sung.

GREETING

The bishop greets the people, using these or other suitable words

Blessed be God, Father, Son and Holy Spirit.
Blessed be his kingdom, now and for ever. Amen.

or from Easter Day to Pentecost
Alleluia Christ is risen.
He is risen indeed. Alleluia.

There is one body and one spirit.
There is one hope to which we were called;
one Lord, one faith, one baptism,
one God and Father of all.

Peace be with you.
And also with you.

The bishop may introduce the service.

Gloria in Excelsis may be used.

COLLECT

The bishop introduces a period of silent prayer with the words
Let us pray *or a more specific bidding.*

The collect of the day is normally used on Sundays and on principal festivals. On other occasions a seasonal collect from the appendices to the service for Holy Baptism *or this prayer is used*

> Heavenly Father,
> by the power of your Holy Spirit
> you give to your faithful people new life in the
>   water of baptism.
> Guide and strengthen us by the same Spirit,
> that we who are born again may serve you in
>   faith and love,
> and grow into the full stature of your Son, Jesus Christ,
> who is alive and reigns with you in the unity
>   of the Holy Spirit
> now and for ever. **Amen.**

Liturgy of the Word

The readings of the day are normally used on Sundays and principal festivals. For other occasions a Table of Readings is provided in the Appendix.

Either one or two readings from scripture precede the gospel reading. At the end of each the reader may say

> This is the word of the Lord.
> **Thanks be to God.**

The psalm or canticle follows the first reading; other hymns and songs may be used between the readings.

GOSPEL READING

An acclamation may herald the gospel reading.

When the gospel is announced the reader says

Hear the gospel of our Lord Jesus Christ according to *N*.
Glory to you, O Lord.

At the end

This is the gospel of the Lord.
Praise to you, O Christ.

SERMON

Liturgy of Initiation

PRESENTATION OF THE CANDIDATES

The candidates are presented to the congregation. Where appropriate, they are presented by their godparents or sponsors. If there are infants for baptism, the direction in Note 1 is followed.

The bishop asks those who are candidates for baptism

Do you wish to be baptized?
I do.

The bishop asks the candidates for confirmation who have been baptized (together with those who wish to affirm their baptismal faith and/or those who are to be received into the communion of the Church of England)

Have you been baptized in the name of the Father, and of the Son, and of the Holy Spirit?
I have.

The bishop asks all the candidates

Are you ready with your own mouth and from your own heart to affirm your faith in Jesus Christ?
I am.

Testimony by the candidates may follow.

The bishop addresses the whole congregation

Faith is the gift of God to his people.
In baptism the Lord is adding to our number those whom
he is calling.
People of God, will you welcome *these candidates* and
uphold *them* in *their* life in Christ?
With the help of God, we will.

*If children are to be baptized, the questions to parents and
godparents in the service for* Holy Baptism *are used.*

DECISION

A large candle may be lit. The bishop addresses all the candidates

In baptism, God calls us out of darkness into his
marvellous light.
To follow Christ means dying to sin and rising to
new life with him.
Therefore I ask:

Do you reject the devil and all rebellion against God?
I reject them.
Do you renounce the deceit and corruption of evil?
I renounce them.
Do you repent of the sins that separate us from
God and neighbour?
I repent of them.

Do you turn to Christ as Saviour?
I turn to Christ.
Do you submit to Christ as Lord?
I submit to Christ.
Do you come to Christ, the way, the truth and the life?
I come to Christ.

SIGNING WITH THE CROSS

*The bishop or another minister makes the sign of the cross on the
forehead of each candidate for baptism, saying*

Christ claims you for his own.
Receive the sign of his cross.

The bishop may invite their sponsors to sign the candidates with the sign of the cross.

When all the candidates for baptism have been signed, the bishop says to them

> Do not be ashamed to confess the faith of Christ crucified.
> **Fight valiantly as a disciple of Christ**
> **against sin, the world and the devil,**
> **and remain faithful to Christ to the end of your life.**

The bishop says

> May almighty God deliver you from the
>   powers of darkness,
> restore in you the image of his glory,
> and lead you in the light and obedience of Christ. **Amen.**

> *or when there are no candidates for baptism he may say*
> May God who has given you the desire to
>   follow Christ
> give you strength to continue in the Way. **Amen.**

PRAYER OVER THE WATER

The ministers and candidates for baptism, together with candidates for confirmation, affirmation of baptismal faith and reception into the communion of the Church of England, gather at the baptismal font. A canticle, psalm, hymn or a litany may be used.

When there are candidates for baptism, the bishop stands before the water of baptism and says (optional seasonal and responsive forms are provided in the appendices to the service for Holy Baptism)

> Praise God who made heaven and earth,
> **who keeps his promise for ever.**

> Let us give thanks to the Lord our God.
> **It is right to give him thanks and praise.**

> We thank you, almighty God, for the gift of water
> to sustain, refresh and cleanse all life.
> Over water the Holy Spirit moved in the
>   beginning of creation.

Through water you led the children of Israel
from slavery in Egypt to freedom in the promised land.
In water your Son Jesus received the baptism of John
and was anointed by the Holy Spirit as the Messiah,
    the Christ,
to lead us from the death of sin to newness of life.

We thank you, Father, for the water of baptism.
In it we are buried with Christ in his death.
By it we share in his resurrection.
Through it we are reborn by the Holy Spirit.
Therefore, in joyful obedience to your Son,
we baptize into his fellowship those who come
    to him in faith.

Now sanctify this water that, by the power of
    your Holy Spirit,
they may be cleansed from sin and born again.
Renewed in your image, may they walk by the
    light of faith
and continue for ever in the risen life of Jesus Christ
    our Lord;
to whom with you and the Holy Spirit
be all honour and glory, now and for ever. **Amen.**

PROFESSION OF FAITH

The bishop addresses the congregation

Brothers and sisters, I ask you to profess
together with *these candidates*
the faith of the Church.

Do you believe and trust in God the Father?
**I believe in God, the Father almighty,
creator of heaven and earth.**

Do you believe and trust in his Son Jesus Christ?
**I believe in Jesus Christ, his only Son, our Lord,
who was conceived by the Holy Spirit,
born of the Virgin Mary,
suffered under Pontius Pilate,
was crucified, died, and was buried;**

he descended to the dead.
On the third day he rose again;
he ascended into heaven,
he is seated at the right hand of the Father,
and he will come to judge the living
    and the dead.

Do you believe and trust in the Holy Spirit?
I believe in the Holy Spirit,
the holy catholic Church,
the communion of saints,
the forgiveness of sins,
the resurrection of the body,
and the life everlasting. Amen.

BAPTISM

The bishop may address each candidate for baptism by name, saying
    N, is this your faith?

and candidates answer in their own words, or
This is my faith.

The bishop or another minister dips each candidate in water, or pours water on them, saying
    N, I baptize you
    in the name of the Father,
    and of the Son,
    and of the Holy Spirit. **Amen.**

If the newly baptized are clothed with a white robe, a hymn or song may be used, and a minister may say
You have been clothed with Christ.
As many as are baptized into Christ have put
    on Christ.

If those who have been baptized were not signed with the cross immediately after the Decision, the bishop signs each one now.

> May God, who has received you by baptism
>   into his Church,
> pour upon you the riches of his grace,
> that within the company of Christ's pilgrim people
> you may daily be renewed by his anointing Spirit,
> and come to the inheritance of the saints in glory. **Amen.**

DECLARATION FOR AFFIRMATION

*Those who are to affirm their baptismal faith stand before the bishop,
who says*

> I call upon those who are affirming their baptismal faith
> to renew their commitment to Jesus Christ.

These candidates face the people and make this declaration

> **I answer the call of God my creator.**
> **I trust in Jesus Christ as my Saviour.**
> **I seek new life from the Holy Spirit.**

The congregation responds

> **God, who has called you, is faithful.**
> **Rejoice in your baptism into Jesus Christ.**
> **Walk with us in the life of the Spirit.**

DECLARATION FOR RECEPTION

*Those who are to be received into the communion of the Church of
England stand before the bishop to make this declaration.*

The bishop says

> You are here to be received into the communion of the
> Church of England.

> Do you acknowledge the Church of England as part of the
> one, holy, catholic and apostolic Church?
> **I do.**

> Do you accept the teaching, discipline and authority of
> the Church of England?
> **I do.**

Will you take part with us in worship and mission?
I will.

The candidates for confirmation who have previously been baptized (together with those affirming their baptismal faith or seeking reception) may come forward to the font and sign themselves with water, or the bishop may sprinkle them.

Then the bishop says

Almighty God,
we thank you for our fellowship in the household of faith
with all who have been baptized into your name.
Keep us faithful to our baptism,
and so make us ready for that day
when the whole creation shall be made perfect
    in your Son,
our Saviour Jesus Christ. **Amen.**

The bishop and the candidates gather at the place of confirmation. A hymn, chant or litany may be used.

CONFIRMATION

The bishop stands before those who are to be confirmed, and says

Our help is in the name of the Lord
who has made heaven and earth.

Blessed be the name of the Lord
now and for ever. Amen.

The bishop extends his hands towards those to be confirmed and says

Almighty and ever-living God,
you have given these your servants new birth
in baptism by water and the Spirit,
and have forgiven them all their sins.
Let your Holy Spirit rest upon them:
the Spirit of wisdom and understanding;
the Spirit of counsel and inward strength;
the Spirit of knowledge and true godliness;
and let their delight be in the fear of the Lord. **Amen.**

The bishop addresses each candidate by name

N, God has called you by name and made you his own.

He then lays his hand on the head of each, saying

Confirm, O Lord, your servant with your Holy Spirit.
Amen.

AFFIRMATION OF BAPTISMAL FAITH

The bishop extends his hands towards those who seek to affirm their baptismal faith and says

God of mercy and love,
in baptism you welcome the sinner
and restore the dead to life.
You create a clean heart in those who repent,
and give your Holy Spirit to those who ask.
Grant that these your servants may grow
into the fullness of the stature of Christ.
Equip them with the gifts of your Holy Spirit,
and fill them with faith in Jesus Christ
and with love for all your people,
in the service of your kingdom. **Amen.**

The bishop lays his hand on each one, saying

N, may God renew his life within you
that you may confess his name this day and for ever.
Amen.

RECEPTION INTO THE COMMUNION OF THE CHURCH OF ENGLAND

The bishop extends his hands towards those who are to be received and says

God of mercy and love,
by one Spirit we have all been baptized into one body
and made to drink of the one Spirit;
we thank you for the gifts you have given to these
    your servants
for the building up of the body of Christ.

Grant that they may continue in the life of the Spirit
and walk with us in the light and obedience of Christ.
By the same Spirit, fill the whole Church
with your overflowing love;
give us knowledge and discernment of your will,
and steadfastness in your service,
until we all come to the unity of the faith,
to the measure of the full stature of Christ,
through whom we make our prayer. **Amen.**

The bishop takes the hand of each person to be received, saying

N, we recognize you as a member of the one, holy,
catholic and apostolic Church;
and we receive you into the communion of the
Church of England
in the name of the Father, and of the Son, and of
the Holy Spirit. **Amen.**

*The bishop invites the congregation to pray for all those on whom
hands have been laid*

**Defend, O Lord, these your servants with your
heavenly grace,
that they may continue yours for ever,
and daily increase in your Holy Spirit more and more
until they come to your everlasting kingdom. Amen.**

COMMISSION

The bishop may use this Commission

Those who are baptized are called to worship
and serve God.

Will you continue in the apostles' teaching
and fellowship,
in the breaking of bread, and in the prayers?
With the help of God, I will.

Will you persevere in resisting evil,
and, whenever you fall into sin, repent and return
to the Lord?
With the help of God, I will.

Will you proclaim by word and example
the good news of God in Christ?
With the help of God, I will.

Will you seek and serve Christ in all people,
loving your neighbour as yourself?
With the help of God, I will.

Will you acknowledge Christ's authority over
  human society,
by prayer for the world and its leaders,
by defending the weak, and by seeking peace and justice?
With the help of God, I will.

May Christ dwell in your hearts through faith,
that you may be rooted and grounded in love
and bring forth the fruit of the Spirit. **Amen.**

The Prayers of Intercession may follow. It is appropriate that the newly baptized and confirmed take their part in leading the prayers. The prayers provided in the service for Holy Baptism *may be used. If the rest of the Eucharist does not follow, these prayers may be used after the Welcome and Peace.*

WELCOME AND PEACE

The bishop addresses the newly baptized

There is one Lord, one faith, one baptism.
N and *N*, by one Spirit we are all baptized
  into one body.
We welcome you in the fellowship of faith;
we are children of the same heavenly Father;
we welcome you.

The congregation may greet the newly baptized.

The bishop introduces the Peace in these or other suitable words (seasonal forms are provided in Appendix 2 of the service for Holy Baptism)

God has made us one in Christ.
He has set his seal upon us
and, as a pledge of what is to come,
has given the Spirit to dwell in our hearts.

The peace of the Lord be always with you.
And also with you.

A minister may say

Let us offer one another a sign of peace.

All may exchange a sign of peace.

If the Liturgy of the Eucharist does not follow immediately, the service concludes with suitable prayers, ending with the Lord's Prayer and the Sending Out.

Liturgy of the Eucharist

The Eucharist continues with

PREPARATION OF THE TABLE

TAKING OF THE BREAD AND WINE

EUCHARISTIC PRAYER

This proper preface may be used

And now we give you thanks
because by water and the Holy Spirit
you have made us a holy people in Jesus Christ our Lord;
you raise us to new life in him
and renew in us the image of your glory.

LORD'S PRAYER

BREAKING OF THE BREAD

GIVING OF THE BREAD AND WINE

PRAYER AFTER COMMUNION

The authorized post communion prayer for the day is normally used on Sundays and on principal festivals. On other occasions a seasonal prayer from Appendix 2 of the service for Holy Baptism *or this prayer is used*

> God of mercy,
> by whose grace alone we are accepted
> and equipped for your service:
> stir up in us the gifts of your Holy Spirit
> and make us worthy of our calling;
> that we may bring forth the fruit of the Spirit
> in love and joy and peace;
> through Jesus Christ our Lord. **Amen.**

Sending Out

BLESSING

The bishop may use a seasonal blessing (Appendix 2 of the service for Holy Baptism*), or another suitable blessing, or*

> The God of all grace,
> who called you to his eternal glory in Christ Jesus,
> establish, strengthen and settle you in the faith;
> and the blessing of God almighty,
> the Father, the Son and the Holy Spirit,
> be upon you and remain with you always. **Amen.**

GIVING OF A LIGHTED CANDLE

A hymn may be sung.

The bishop or another person may give all candidates a lighted candle. These candles may be lit from the candle used at the Decision.

When all have received a candle, the bishop says

God has delivered us from the dominion of darkness
and has given us a place with the saints in light.

You have received the light of Christ;
walk in this light all the days of your life.
**Shine as a light in the world
to the glory of God the Father.**

DISMISSAL

Go in the light and peace of Christ.
Thanks be to God.

From Easter to Pentecost **Alleluia Alleluia** *may be added after both
the versicle and response.*

*The bishop may lead the newly baptized and confirmed through the
church.*

The Eucharist with Baptism and Confirmation together with Affirmation of Baptismal Faith and Reception into the Communion of the Church of England

Versions of this service are shown in outline form below and in detail on pages 122-83.

The service if there are no candidates for baptism

In the **PRESENTATION OF THE CANDIDATES**

OMIT   *The bishop asks those who are candidates for baptism*

Do you wish to be baptized?
I do.

In the **DECISION**

USE   *The bishop says*

May God, who has given you the desire to follow Christ, give you also strength to continue in the Way. **Amen.**

OMIT   **SIGNING WITH THE CROSS**

OMIT   **PRAYER OVER THE WATER**

OMIT   **BAPTISM**

OMIT   **WELCOME**

The service if there are no candidates for confirmation

OMIT **CONFIRMATION**

The service if there are no persons affirming their baptismal faith

OMIT **DECLARATION FOR AFFIRMATION**

OMIT **AFFIRMATION OF BAPTISMAL FAITH** *after Confirmation*

The service if there are no persons to be received into the communion of the Church of England

OMIT **DECLARATION FOR RECEPTION**

OMIT **RECEPTION INTO THE COMMUNION OF THE CHURCH OF ENGLAND** *after Confirmation*

The service if the Liturgy of the Eucharist does not follow immediately

One or more of the following prayers may be used at the Prayers of Intercession

(by the bishop)

Heavenly Father, we pray for *these your servants*
upon whom we have now laid our hands after the
example of the apostles.
Assure *them* by this sign of your favour towards *them;*
may your fatherly hand ever be over *them,*
your Holy Spirit ever be with *them;*

strengthen *them* continually with the Body and Blood
of your Son,
and so lead *them* in the knowledge and obedience
of your word,
that *they* may ever hold fast the blessed hope of
everlasting life;
through Jesus Christ our Lord. **Amen.**

Almighty God,
whose Holy Spirit equips the Church with a rich
variety of gifts,
grant that we may use them to bear witness to Christ
by lives built on faith and love.
Make us ready to live his gospel and eager to do his will,
that we may share with all your Church in the joys of
eternal life;
through Jesus Christ our Lord. **Amen.**

Lord, make us instruments of your peace.
Where there is hatred, let us sow love;
where there is injury, let there be pardon;
where there is discord, union;
where there is doubt, faith;
where there is despair, hope;
where there is darkness, light;
where there is sadness, joy;
for your mercy and for your truth's sake. Amen.

Thanks be to you, Lord Jesus Christ,
for all the benefits that you have won for us,
for all the pains and insults you have borne for us.
Most merciful redeemer,
friend and brother,
may we know you more clearly,
love you more dearly,
and follow you more nearly,
day by day. Amen.

Eternal God,
you have declared in Christ
the completion of your purpose of love.
May we live by faith, walk in hope,
and be renewed in love,
until the world reflects your glory,
and you are all in all.
Even so; come, Lord Jesus. Amen.

Then all say the Lord's Prayer.

The service concludes with the Sending Out.

Baptism and Confirmation at the Eucharist

Preparation

At the entry of the ministers, a hymn may be sung.

GREETING

The bishop greets the people, using these or other suitable words

Blessed be God, Father, Son and Holy Spirit.
Blessed be his kingdom, now and for ever. Amen.

> *or from Easter Day to Pentecost*
> Alleluia Christ is risen.
> **He is risen indeed. Alleluia.**

There is one body and one spirit.
There is one hope to which we were called;
one Lord, one faith, one baptism,
one God and Father of all.

Peace be with you.
And also with you.

The bishop may introduce the service.

Gloria in Excelsis may be used.

COLLECT

The bishop introduces a period of silent prayer with the words
Let us pray *or a more specific bidding.*

The collect of the day is normally used on Sundays and on principal festivals. On other occasions a seasonal collect from the appendices to the service for Holy Baptism *or this prayer is used*

> Heavenly Father,
> by the power of your Holy Spirit
> you give to your faithful people new life in the
>   water of baptism.
> Guide and strengthen us by the same Spirit,
> that we who are born again may serve you in
>   faith and love,
> and grow into the full stature of your Son, Jesus Christ,
> who is alive and reigns with you in the unity of
>   the Holy Spirit
> now and for ever. **Amen.**

Liturgy of the Word

The readings of the day are normally used on Sundays and principal festivals. For other occasions a Table of Readings is provided in the Appendix.

Either one or two readings from scripture precede the gospel reading. At the end of each the reader may say

> This is the word of the Lord.
> **Thanks be to God.**

The psalm or canticle follows the first reading; other hymns and songs may be used between the readings.

GOSPEL READING

An acclamation may herald the gospel reading.

When the gospel is announced the reader says

> Hear the gospel of our Lord Jesus Christ according to *N.*
> **Glory to you, O Lord.**

At the end

This is the gospel of the Lord.
Praise to you, O Christ.

SERMON

Liturgy of Initiation

PRESENTATION OF THE CANDIDATES

The candidates are presented to the congregation. Where appropriate, they are presented by their godparents or sponsors. If there are infants for baptism, the direction in Note 1 is followed.

The bishop asks those who are candidates for baptism

Do you wish to be baptized?
I do.

The bishop asks the candidates for confirmation who have been baptized

Have you been baptized in the name of the Father, and of the Son, and of the Holy Spirit?
I have.

The bishop asks all the candidates

Are you ready with your own mouth and from your own heart to affirm your faith in Jesus Christ?
I am.

Testimony by the candidates may follow.

The bishop addresses the whole congregation

Faith is the gift of God to his people.
In baptism the Lord is adding to our number those whom
    he is calling.

People of God, will you welcome *these candidates* and
　　uphold *them* in *their* life in Christ?
With the help of God, we will.

*If children are to be baptized, the questions to parents and
godparents in the service for* Holy Baptism *are used.*

DECISION

A large candle may be lit. The bishop addresses all the candidates

In baptism, God calls us out of darkness into his
　　marvellous light.
To follow Christ means dying to sin and rising to
　　new life with him.
Therefore I ask:

Do you reject the devil and all rebellion against God?
I reject them.
Do you renounce the deceit and corruption of evil?
I renounce them.
Do you repent of the sins that separate us from
　　God and neighbour?
I repent of them.

Do you turn to Christ as Saviour?
I turn to Christ.
Do you submit to Christ as Lord?
I submit to Christ.
Do you come to Christ, the way, the truth and the life?
I come to Christ.

SIGNING WITH THE CROSS

*The bishop or another minister makes the sign of the cross on the
forehead of each candidate for baptism, saying*

Christ claims you for his own.
Receive the sign of his cross.

*The bishop may invite their sponsors to sign the candidates with the
sign of the cross.*

When all the candidates for baptism have been signed, the bishop says to them

> Do not be ashamed to confess the faith of Christ crucified.
> **Fight valiantly as a disciple of Christ**
> **against sin, the world and the devil,**
> **and remain faithful to Christ to the end of your life.**

The bishop says

> May almighty God deliver you from the
>   powers of darkness,
> restore in you the image of his glory,
> and lead you in the light and obedience of Christ. **Amen.**

PRAYER OVER THE WATER

The ministers and candidates for baptism and confirmation gather at the baptismal font. A canticle, psalm, hymn or a litany may be used.

The bishop stands before the water of baptism and says (optional seasonal and responsive forms are provided in the appendices to the service for Holy Baptism*)*

> Praise God who made heaven and earth,
> **who keeps his promise for ever.**
>
> Let us give thanks to the Lord our God.
> **It is right to give him thanks and praise.**
>
> We thank you, almighty God, for the gift of water
> to sustain, refresh and cleanse all life.
> Over water the Holy Spirit moved in the
>   beginning of creation.
> Through water you led the children of Israel
> from slavery in Egypt to freedom in the promised land.
> In water your Son Jesus received the baptism of John
> and was anointed by the Holy Spirit as the Messiah,
>   the Christ,
> to lead us from the death of sin to newness of life.
>
> We thank you, Father, for the water of baptism.
> In it we are buried with Christ in his death.
> By it we share in his resurrection.

Through it we are reborn by the Holy Spirit.
Therefore, in joyful obedience to your Son,
we baptize into his fellowship those who come
    to him in faith.

Now sanctify this water that, by the power of
    your Holy Spirit,
they may be cleansed from sin and born again.
Renewed in your image, may they walk by the
    light of faith
and continue for ever in the risen life of Jesus Christ
    our Lord;
to whom with you and the Holy Spirit
be all honour and glory, now and for ever. **Amen.**

PROFESSION OF FAITH

The bishop addresses the congregation

Brothers and sisters, I ask you to profess
together with *these candidates*
the faith of the Church.

Do you believe and trust in God the Father?
I believe in God, the Father almighty,
creator of heaven and earth.

Do you believe and trust in his Son Jesus Christ?
I believe in Jesus Christ, his only Son, our Lord,
who was conceived by the Holy Spirit,
born of the Virgin Mary,
suffered under Pontius Pilate,
was crucified, died, and was buried;
he descended to the dead.
On the third day he rose again;
he ascended into heaven,
he is seated at the right hand of the Father,
and he will come to judge the living
    and the dead.

Do you believe and trust in the Holy Spirit?
I believe in the Holy Spirit,
the holy catholic Church,
the communion of saints,
the forgiveness of sins,
the resurrection of the body,
and the life everlasting. Amen.

BAPTISM

The bishop may address each candidate for baptism by
name, saying
N, is this your faith?

and candidates answer in their own words, or
This is my faith.

The bishop or another minister dips each candidate in water, or pours
water on them, saying
N, I baptize you
in the name of the Father,
and of the Son,
and of the Holy Spirit. **Amen.**

If the newly baptized are clothed with a white robe, a hymn
or song may be used, and a minister may say
You have been clothed with Christ.
As many as are baptized into Christ have put
on Christ.

If those who have been baptized were not signed with the
cross immediately after the Decision, the bishop signs each
one now.

The bishop says
May God, who has received you by baptism
into his Church,
pour upon you the riches of his grace,
that within the company of Christ's pilgrim people
you may daily be renewed by his anointing Spirit,
and come to the inheritance of the saints in glory. **Amen.**

The candidates for confirmation who have previously been baptized may come forward to the font and sign themselves with water, or the bishop may sprinkle them.

Then the bishop says

> Almighty God,
> we thank you for our fellowship in the household of faith
> with all who have been baptized into your name.
> Keep us faithful to our baptism,
> and so make us ready for that day
> when the whole creation shall be made perfect
>   in your Son,
> our Saviour Jesus Christ. **Amen.**

The bishop and the candidates gather at the place of confirmation. A hymn, chant or litany may be used.

CONFIRMATION

The bishop stands before those who are to be confirmed, and says

> Our help is in the name of the Lord
> **who has made heaven and earth.**
>
> Blessed be the name of the Lord
> **now and for ever. Amen.**

The bishop extends his hands towards those to be confirmed and says

> Almighty and ever-living God,
> you have given these your servants new birth
> in baptism by water and the Spirit,
> and have forgiven them all their sins.
> Let your Holy Spirit rest upon them:
> the Spirit of wisdom and understanding;
> the Spirit of counsel and inward strength;
> the Spirit of knowledge and true godliness;
> and let their delight be in the fear of the Lord. **Amen.**

The bishop addresses each candidate by name

N, God has called you by name and made you his own.

He then lays his hand on the head of each, saying

Confirm, O Lord, your servant with your Holy Spirit.
Amen.

The bishop invites the congregation to pray for all those on whom hands have been laid

**Defend, O Lord, these your servants with your
   heavenly grace,
that they may continue yours for ever,
and daily increase in your Holy Spirit more and more
until they come to your everlasting kingdom. Amen.**

COMMISSION

The bishop may use this Commission

Those who are baptized are called to worship
   and serve God.

Will you continue in the apostles' teaching
   and fellowship,
in the breaking of bread, and in the prayers?
With the help of God, I will.

Will you persevere in resisting evil,
and, whenever you fall into sin, repent and return
   to the Lord?
With the help of God, I will.

Will you proclaim by word and example
the good news of God in Christ?
With the help of God, I will.

Will you seek and serve Christ in all people,
loving your neighbour as yourself?
With the help of God, I will.

Will you acknowledge Christ's authority over
    human society,
by prayer for the world and its leaders,
by defending the weak, and by seeking peace and justice?
With the help of God, I will.

May Christ dwell in your hearts through faith,
that you may be rooted and grounded in love
and bring forth the fruit of the Spirit. **Amen.**

*The Prayers of Intercession may follow. It is appropriate that the newly
baptized and confirmed take their part in leading the prayers. The
prayers provided in the service for* Holy Baptism *may be used.*

WELCOME AND PEACE

The bishop addresses the newly baptized

There is one Lord, one faith, one baptism.
N and N, by one Spirit we are all baptized into one body.
We welcome you in the fellowship of faith;
we are children of the same heavenly Father;
we welcome you.

The congregation may greet the newly baptized.

*The bishop introduces the Peace in these or other suitable words
(seasonal forms are provided in Appendix 2 of the service for* Holy
Baptism*)*

God has made us one in Christ.
He has set his seal upon us
and, as a pledge of what is to come,
has given the Spirit to dwell in our hearts.

The peace of the Lord be always with you.
And also with you.

> *A minister may say*
> Let us offer one another a sign of peace.
> *All may exchange a sign of peace.*

Liturgy of the Eucharist

The Eucharist continues with

PREPARATION OF THE TABLE

TAKING OF THE BREAD AND WINE

EUCHARISTIC PRAYER

This proper preface may be used

> And now we give you thanks
> because by water and the Holy Spirit
> you have made us a holy people in Jesus Christ our Lord;
> you raise us to new life in him
> and renew in us the image of your glory.

LORD'S PRAYER

BREAKING OF THE BREAD

GIVING OF THE BREAD AND WINE

PRAYER AFTER COMMUNION

The authorized post communion prayer for the day is normally used on Sundays and on principal festivals. On other occasions a seasonal prayer from Appendix 2 of the service for Holy Baptism *or this prayer is used*

> God of mercy,
> by whose grace alone we are accepted
> and equipped for your service:
> stir up in us the gifts of your Holy Spirit
> and make us worthy of our calling;
> that we may bring forth the fruit of the Spirit
> in love and joy and peace;
> through Jesus Christ our Lord. **Amen.**

Sending Out

BLESSING

The bishop may use a seasonal blessing (Appendix 2 of the service for Holy Baptism), or another suitable blessing, or

> The God of all grace,
> who called you to his eternal glory in Christ Jesus,
> establish, strengthen and settle you in the faith;
> and the blessing of God almighty,
> the Father, the Son and the Holy Spirit,
> be upon you and remain with you always. **Amen.**

GIVING OF A LIGHTED CANDLE

A hymn may be sung.

The bishop or another person may give all candidates a lighted candle. These candles may be lit from the candle used at the Decision.

When all have received a candle, the bishop says

> God has delivered us from the dominion of darkness
> and has given us a place with the saints in light.

> You have received the light of Christ;
> walk in this light all the days of your life.
> **Shine as a light in the world**
> **to the glory of God the Father.**

DISMISSAL

> Go in the light and peace of Christ.
> **Thanks be to God.**

From Easter to Pentecost **Alleluia Alleluia** *may be added after both the versicle and response.*

The bishop may lead the newly baptized and confirmed through the church.

Confirmation at the Eucharist

Preparation

At the entry of the ministers, a hymn may be sung.

GREETING

The bishop greets the people, using these or other suitable words

Blessed be God, Father, Son and Holy Spirit.
Blessed be his kingdom, now and for ever. Amen.

or from Easter Day to Pentecost

Alleluia Christ is risen.
He is risen indeed. Alleluia.

There is one body and one spirit.
There is one hope to which we were called;
one Lord, one faith, one baptism,
one God and Father of all.

Peace be with you.
And also with you.

The bishop may introduce the service.

Gloria in Excelsis may be used.

COLLECT

The bishop introduces a period of silent prayer with the words
Let us pray *or a more specific bidding.*

The collect of the day is normally used on Sundays and on principal festivals. On other occasions a seasonal collect from the appendices to the service for Holy Baptism *or this prayer is used*

Heavenly Father,
by the power of your Holy Spirit
you give to your faithful people new life in the
    water of baptism.
Guide and strengthen us by the same Spirit,
that we who are born again may serve you in
    faith and love,
and grow into the full stature of your Son, Jesus Christ,
who is alive and reigns with you in the unity of
    the Holy Spirit
now and for ever. **Amen.**

Liturgy of the Word

The readings of the day are normally used on Sundays and principal festivals. For other occasions a Table of Readings is provided in the Appendix.

Either one or two readings from scripture precede the gospel reading. At the end of each the reader may say

This is the word of the Lord.
Thanks be to God.

The psalm or canticle follows the first reading; other hymns and songs may be used between the readings.

GOSPEL READING
An acclamation may herald the gospel reading.

When the gospel is announced the reader says

Hear the gospel of our Lord Jesus Christ according to *N.*
Glory to you, O Lord.

This is the gospel of the Lord.
Praise to you, O Christ.

SERMON

Liturgy of Initiation

PRESENTATION OF THE CANDIDATES

The candidates are presented to the congregation. Where appropriate, they are presented by their godparents or sponsors.

The bishop asks the candidates

Have you been baptized in the name of the Father, and of the Son, and of the Holy Spirit?
I have.

Are you ready with your own mouth and from your own heart to affirm your faith in Jesus Christ?
I am.

Testimony by the candidates may follow.

The bishop addresses the whole congregation

People of God, will you welcome *these candidates* and uphold *them* in *their* life in Christ?
With the help of God, we will.

DECISION

A large candle may be lit. The bishop addresses all the candidates

In baptism, God calls us out of darkness into his marvellous light.
To follow Christ means dying to sin and rising to new life with him.
Therefore I ask:

Do you reject the devil and all rebellion against God?
I reject them.
Do you renounce the deceit and corruption of evil?
I renounce them.
Do you repent of the sins that separate us from
    God and neighbour?
I repent of them.

Do you turn to Christ as Saviour?
I turn to Christ.
Do you submit to Christ as Lord?
I submit to Christ.
Do you come to Christ, the way, the truth and the life?
I come to Christ.

The bishop says

May God who has given you the desire to follow Christ
give you strength to continue in the Way. **Amen.**

*The ministers and candidates for confirmation gather at the baptismal
font. A canticle, psalm, hymn or a litany may be used.*

PROFESSION OF FAITH

The bishop addresses the congregation

Brothers and sisters, I ask you to profess
together with *these candidates*
the faith of the Church.

Do you believe and trust in God the Father?
I believe in God, the Father almighty,
creator of heaven and earth.

Do you believe and trust in his Son Jesus Christ?
I believe in Jesus Christ, his only Son, our Lord,
who was conceived by the Holy Spirit,
born of the Virgin Mary,
suffered under Pontius Pilate,
was crucified, died, and was buried;
he descended to the dead.

On the third day he rose again;
he ascended into heaven,
he is seated at the right hand of the Father,
and he will come to judge the living
and the dead.

Do you believe and trust in the Holy Spirit?
**I believe in the Holy Spirit,
the holy catholic Church,
the communion of saints,
the forgiveness of sins,
the resurrection of the body,
and the life everlasting. Amen.**

*The candidates may come forward to the font and sign themselves
with water, or the bishop may sprinkle them.*

Then the bishop says

Almighty God,
we thank you for our fellowship in the household of faith
with all who have been baptized into your name.
Keep us faithful to our baptism,
and so make us ready for that day
when the whole creation shall be made perfect
in your Son,
our Saviour Jesus Christ. **Amen.**

*The bishop and the candidates gather at the place of confirmation. A
hymn, chant or litany may be used.*

CONFIRMATION

The bishop stands before those who are to be confirmed, and says

Our help is in the name of the Lord
who has made heaven and earth.

Blessed be the name of the Lord
now and for ever. Amen.

The bishop extends his hands towards those to be confirmed and says

Almighty and ever-living God,
you have given these your servants new birth
in baptism by water and the Spirit,
and have forgiven them all their sins.
Let your Holy Spirit rest upon them:
the Spirit of wisdom and understanding;
the Spirit of counsel and inward strength;
the Spirit of knowledge and true godliness;
and let their delight be in the fear of the Lord. **Amen.**

The bishop addresses each candidate by name

N, God has called you by name and made you his own.

He then lays his hand on the head of each, saying

Confirm, O Lord, your servant with your Holy Spirit.
Amen.

The bishop invites the congregation to pray for all those on whom hands have been laid

**Defend, O Lord, these your servants with your
 heavenly grace,
that they may continue yours for ever,
and daily increase in your Holy Spirit more and more
until they come to your everlasting kingdom. Amen.**

COMMISSION

The bishop may use this Commission

Those who are baptized are called to worship and
 serve God.

Will you continue in the apostles' teaching
 and fellowship,
in the breaking of bread, and in the prayers?
With the help of God, I will.

Will you persevere in resisting evil,
and, whenever you fall into sin, repent and return
 to the Lord?
With the help of God, I will.

Will you proclaim by word and example
the good news of God in Christ?
With the help of God, I will.

Will you seek and serve Christ in all people,
loving your neighbour as yourself?
With the help of God, I will.

Will you acknowledge Christ's authority over
    human society,
by prayer for the world and its leaders,
by defending the weak, and by seeking peace and justice?
With the help of God, I will.

May Christ dwell in your hearts through faith,
that you may be rooted and grounded in love
and bring forth the fruit of the Spirit. **Amen.**

The Prayers of Intercession may follow. It is appropriate that the newly confirmed take their part in leading the prayers. The prayers provided in the service for Holy Baptism *may be used.*

PEACE

The bishop introduces the Peace in these or other suitable words (seasonal forms are provided in Appendix 2 of the service for Holy Baptism)

God has made us one in Christ.
He has set his seal upon us
and, as a pledge of what is to come,
has given the Spirit to dwell in our hearts.

The peace of the Lord be always with you.
And also with you.

> *A minister may say*
> Let us offer one another a sign of peace.
> *All may exchange a sign of peace.*

Liturgy of the Eucharist

The Eucharist continues with

PREPARATION OF THE TABLE

TAKING OF THE BREAD AND WINE

EUCHARISTIC PRAYER

This proper preface may be used

> And now we give you thanks
> because by water and the Holy Spirit
> you have made us a holy people in Jesus Christ our Lord;
> you raise us to new life in him
> and renew in us the image of your glory.

LORD'S PRAYER

BREAKING OF THE BREAD

GIVING OF THE BREAD AND WINE

PRAYER AFTER COMMUNION

The authorized post communion prayer for the day is normally used on Sundays and on principal festivals. On other occasions a seasonal prayer from Appendix 2 of the service for Holy Baptism *or this prayer is used*

> God of mercy,
> by whose grace alone we are accepted
> and equipped for your service:
> stir up in us the gifts of your Holy Spirit
> and make us worthy of our calling;
> that we may bring forth the fruit of the Spirit
> in love and joy and peace;
> through Jesus Christ our Lord. **Amen.**

Sending Out

BLESSING

*The bishop may use a seasonal blessing (Appendix 2 of the service for
Holy Baptism), or another suitable blessing, or*

> The God of all grace,
> who called you to his eternal glory in Christ Jesus,
> establish, strengthen and settle you in the faith;
> and the blessing of God almighty,
> the Father, the Son and the Holy Spirit,
> be upon you and remain with you always. **Amen.**

DISMISSAL

> Go in the light and peace of Christ.
> **Thanks be to God.**

From Easter to Pentecost **Alleluia Alleluia** *may be added after both
the versicle and response.*

The bishop may lead the newly confirmed through the church.

Baptism and Confirmation outside the Eucharist

Preparation

At the entry of the ministers, a hymn may be sung.

GREETING

The bishop greets the people, using these or other suitable words

Blessed be God, Father, Son and Holy Spirit.
Blessed be his kingdom, now and for ever. Amen.

or from Easter Day to Pentecost
Alleluia Christ is risen.
He is risen indeed. Alleluia.

There is one body and one spirit.
There is one hope to which we were called;
one Lord, one faith, one baptism,
one God and Father of all.

Peace be with you.
And also with you.

The bishop may introduce the service.

Gloria in Excelsis may be used.

COLLECT

The bishop introduces a period of silent prayer with the words
Let us pray *or a more specific bidding.*

The collect of the day is normally used on Sundays and on principal festivals. On other occasions a seasonal collect from the appendices to the service for Holy Baptism *or this prayer is used*

> Heavenly Father,
> by the power of your Holy Spirit
> you give to your faithful people new life in the
>   water of baptism.
> Guide and strengthen us by the same Spirit,
> that we who are born again may serve you in
>   faith and love,
> and grow into the full stature of your Son, Jesus Christ,
> who is alive and reigns with you in the unity of
>   the Holy Spirit
> now and for ever. **Amen.**

Liturgy of the Word

The readings of the day are normally used on Sundays and principal festivals. For other occasions a Table of Readings is provided in the Appendix.

Either one or two readings from scripture precede the gospel reading. At the end of each the reader may say

> This is the word of the Lord.
> **Thanks be to God.**

The psalm or canticle follows the first reading; other hymns and songs may be used between the readings.

GOSPEL READING

An acclamation may herald the gospel reading.

When the gospel is announced the reader says

> Hear the gospel of our Lord Jesus Christ according to *N*.
> **Glory to you, O Lord.**

> This is the gospel of the Lord.
> **Praise to you, O Christ.**

SERMON

Liturgy of Initiation

PRESENTATION OF THE CANDIDATES

The candidates are presented to the congregation. Where appropriate, they are presented by their godparents or sponsors. If there are infants for baptism, the direction in Note 1 is followed.

The bishop asks those who are candidates for baptism

> Do you wish to be baptized?
> **I do.**

The bishop asks the candidates for confirmation who have been baptized

> Have you been baptized in the name of the Father, and of the Son, and of the Holy Spirit?
> **I have.**

The bishop asks all the candidates

> Are you ready with your own mouth and from your own heart to affirm your faith in Jesus Christ?
> **I am.**

Testimony by the candidates may follow.

The bishop addresses the whole congregation

> Faith is the gift of God to his people.
> In baptism the Lord is adding to our number those whom
> he is calling.

People of God, will you welcome *these candidates* and
uphold *them* in *their* life in Christ?
With the help of God, we will.

*If children are to be baptized, the questions to parents and
godparents in the service for* Holy Baptism *are used.*

DECISION

A large candle may be lit. The bishop addresses all the candidates

In baptism, God calls us out of darkness into his
marvellous light.
To follow Christ means dying to sin and rising to
new life with him.
Therefore I ask:

Do you reject the devil and all rebellion against God?
I reject them.
Do you renounce the deceit and corruption of evil?
I renounce them.
Do you repent of the sins that separate us from
God and neighbour?
I repent of them.

Do you turn to Christ as Saviour?
I turn to Christ.
Do you submit to Christ as Lord?
I submit to Christ.
Do you come to Christ, the way, the truth and the life?
I come to Christ.

SIGNING WITH THE CROSS

*The bishop or another minister makes the sign of the cross on the
forehead of each candidate for baptism, saying*

Christ claims you for his own.
Receive the sign of his cross.

*The bishop may invite their sponsors to sign the candidates with the
sign of the cross.*

When all the candidates for baptism have been signed, the bishop says to them

> Do not be ashamed to confess the faith of Christ crucified.
> **Fight valiantly as a disciple of Christ**
> **against sin, the world and the devil,**
> **and remain faithful to Christ to the end of your life.**

The bishop says

> May almighty God deliver you from the
>   powers of darkness,
> restore in you the image of his glory,
> and lead you in the light and obedience of Christ. **Amen.**

PRAYER OVER THE WATER

The ministers and candidates for baptism and confirmation gather at the baptismal font. A canticle, psalm, hymn or a litany may be used.

The bishop stands before the water of baptism and says (optional seasonal and responsive forms are provided in the appendices to the service for Holy Baptism*)*

> Praise God who made heaven and earth,
> **who keeps his promise for ever.**

> Let us give thanks to the Lord our God.
> **It is right to give him thanks and praise.**

> We thank you, almighty God, for the gift of water
> to sustain, refresh and cleanse all life.
> Over water the Holy Spirit moved in the
>   beginning of creation.
> Through water you led the children of Israel
> from slavery in Egypt to freedom in the promised land.
> In water your Son Jesus received the baptism of John
> and was anointed by the Holy Spirit as the Messiah,
>   the Christ,
> to lead us from the death of sin to newness of life.

> We thank you, Father, for the water of baptism.
> In it we are buried with Christ in his death.
> By it we share in his resurrection.

Through it we are reborn by the Holy Spirit.
Therefore, in joyful obedience to your Son,
we baptize into his fellowship those who come
    to him in faith.

Now sanctify this water that, by the power of
    your Holy Spirit,
they may be cleansed from sin and born again.
Renewed in your image, may they walk by the
    light of faith
and continue for ever in the risen life of Jesus Christ
    our Lord;
to whom with you and the Holy Spirit
be all honour and glory, now and for ever. **Amen.**

PROFESSION OF FAITH

The bishop addresses the congregation

Brothers and sisters, I ask you to profess
together with *these candidates*
the faith of the Church.

Do you believe and trust in God the Father?
**I believe in God, the Father almighty,
creator of heaven and earth.**

Do you believe and trust in his Son Jesus Christ?
**I believe in Jesus Christ, his only Son, our Lord,
who was conceived by the Holy Spirit,
born of the Virgin Mary,
suffered under Pontius Pilate,
was crucified, died, and was buried;
he descended to the dead.
On the third day he rose again;
he ascended into heaven,
he is seated at the right hand of the Father,
and he will come to judge the living
    and the dead.**

Do you believe and trust in the Holy Spirit?
I believe in the Holy Spirit,
the holy catholic Church,
the communion of saints,
the forgiveness of sins,
the resurrection of the body,
and the life everlasting. Amen.

BAPTISM

The bishop may address each candidate for baptism by name, saying

N, is this your faith?

and candidates answer in their own words, or
This is my faith.

The bishop or another minister dips each candidate in water, or pours water on them, saying

N, I baptize you
in the name of the Father,
and of the Son,
and of the Holy Spirit. **Amen.**

If the newly baptized are clothed with a white robe, a hymn or song may be used, and a minister may say

You have been clothed with Christ.
As many as are baptized into Christ have put
on Christ.

If those who have been baptized were not signed with the cross immediately after the Decision, the bishop signs each one now.

The bishop says

May God, who has received you by baptism
into his Church,
pour upon you the riches of his grace,
that within the company of Christ's pilgrim people
you may daily be renewed by his anointing Spirit,
and come to the inheritance of the saints in glory. **Amen.**

The candidates for confirmation who have previously been baptized may come forward to the font and sign themselves with water, or the bishop may sprinkle them.

Then the bishop says

Almighty God,
we thank you for our fellowship in the household of faith
with all who have been baptized into your name.
Keep us faithful to our baptism,
and so make us ready for that day
when the whole creation shall be made perfect
     in your Son,
our Saviour Jesus Christ. **Amen.**

The bishop and the candidates gather at the place of confirmation. A hymn, chant or litany may be used.

CONFIRMATION

The bishop stands before those who are to be confirmed, and says

Our help is in the name of the Lord
who has made heaven and earth.

Blessed be the name of the Lord
now and for ever. Amen.

The bishop extends his hands towards those to be confirmed and says

Almighty and ever-living God,
you have given these your servants new birth
in baptism by water and the Spirit,
and have forgiven them all their sins.
Let your Holy Spirit rest upon them:
the Spirit of wisdom and understanding;
the Spirit of counsel and inward strength;
the Spirit of knowledge and true godliness;
and let their delight be in the fear of the Lord. **Amen.**

The bishop addresses each candidate by name

N, God has called you by name and made you his own.

He then lays his hand on the head of each, saying

Confirm, O Lord, your servant with your Holy Spirit.
Amen.

The bishop invites the congregation to pray for all those on whom hands have been laid

**Defend, O Lord, these your servants with your
   heavenly grace,
that they may continue yours for ever,
and daily increase in your Holy Spirit more and more
until they come to your everlasting kingdom. Amen.**

COMMISSION

The bishop may use this Commission

Those who are baptized are called to worship
   and serve God.

Will you continue in the apostles' teaching
   and fellowship,
in the breaking of bread, and in the prayers?
With the help of God, I will.

Will you persevere in resisting evil,
and, whenever you fall into sin, repent and return
   to the Lord?
With the help of God, I will.

Will you proclaim by word and example
the good news of God in Christ?
With the help of God, I will.

Will you seek and serve Christ in all people,
loving your neighbour as yourself?
With the help of God, I will.

Will you acknowledge Christ's authority over
   human society,
by prayer for the world and its leaders,
by defending the weak, and by seeking peace and justice?
With the help of God, I will.

May Christ dwell in your hearts through faith,
that you may be rooted and grounded in love
and bring forth the fruit of the Spirit. **Amen.**

WELCOME AND PEACE

The bishop addresses the newly baptized

There is one Lord, one faith, one baptism.
N and N, by one Spirit we are all baptized into one body.
We welcome you in the fellowship of faith;
we are children of the same heavenly Father;
we welcome you.

The congregation may greet the newly baptized.

*The bishop introduces the Peace in these or other suitable words
(seasonal forms are provided in Appendix 2 of the service for* Holy
Baptism*)*

God has made us one in Christ.
He has set his seal upon us
and, as a pledge of what is to come,
has given the Spirit to dwell in our hearts.

The peace of the Lord be always with you.
And also with you.

A minister may say
Let us offer one another a sign of peace.

All may exchange a sign of peace.

Prayers

*The service continues with suitable prayers, ending with the Lord's
Prayer. It is appropriate that the newly baptized and confirmed take
their part in leading the prayers. The prayers provided on pages 28-9
or on pages 119-21 may be used.*

Sending Out

BLESSING

The bishop may use a seasonal blessing (Appendix 2 of the service for Holy Baptism), or another suitable blessing, or

The God of all grace,
who called you to his eternal glory in Christ Jesus,
establish, strengthen and settle you in the faith;
and the blessing of God almighty,
the Father, the Son and the Holy Spirit,
be upon you and remain with you always. **Amen.**

GIVING OF A LIGHTED CANDLE

A hymn may be sung.

The bishop or another person may give all candidates a lighted candle. These candles may be lit from the candle used at the Decision.

When all have received a candle, the bishop says

God has delivered us from the dominion of darkness
and has given us a place with the saints in light.

You have received the light of Christ;
walk in this light all the days of your life.
**Shine as a light in the world
to the glory of God the Father.**

DISMISSAL

Go in the light and peace of Christ.
Thanks be to God.

From Easter to Pentecost **Alleluia Alleluia** *may be added after both the versicle and response.*

The bishop may lead the newly baptized and confirmed through the church.

Confirmation outside the Eucharist

Preparation

At the entry of the ministers, a hymn may be sung.

GREETING

The bishop greets the people, using these or other suitable words

Blessed be God, Father, Son and Holy Spirit.
Blessed be his kingdom, now and for ever. Amen.

or from Easter Day to Pentecost
Alleluia Christ is risen.
He is risen indeed. Alleluia.

There is one body and one spirit.
There is one hope to which we were called;
one Lord, one faith, one baptism,
one God and Father of all.

Peace be with you.
And also with you.

The bishop may introduce the service.

Gloria in Excelsis may be used.

COLLECT

The bishop introduces a period of silent prayer with the words
Let us pray *or a more specific bidding.*

The collect of the day is normally used on Sundays and on principal festivals. On other occasions a seasonal collect from the appendices to the service for Holy Baptism *or this prayer is used*

Heavenly Father,
by the power of your Holy Spirit
you give to your faithful people new life in the
    water of baptism.
Guide and strengthen us by the same Spirit,
that we who are born again may serve you in
    faith and love,
and grow into the full stature of your Son, Jesus Christ,
who is alive and reigns with you in the unity of
    the Holy Spirit
now and for ever. **Amen.**

Liturgy of the Word

The readings of the day are normally used on Sundays and principal festivals. For other occasions a Table of Readings is provided in the Appendix.

Either one or two readings from scripture precede the gospel reading. At the end of each the reader may say

This is the word of the Lord.
Thanks be to God.

The psalm or canticle follows the first reading; other hymns and songs may be used between the readings.

GOSPEL READING
An acclamation may herald the gospel reading.

When the gospel is announced the reader says

Hear the gospel of our Lord Jesus Christ according to *N.*
Glory to you, O Lord.

> This is the gospel of the Lord.
> **Praise to you, O Christ.**

SERMON

Liturgy of Initiation

PRESENTATION OF THE CANDIDATES

The candidates are presented to the congregation. Where appropriate, they are presented by their godparents or sponsors.

The bishop asks the candidates

> Have you been baptized in the name of the Father, and of the Son, and of the Holy Spirit?
> **I have.**

> Are you ready with your own mouth and from your own heart to affirm your faith in Jesus Christ?
> **I am.**

Testimony by the candidates may follow.

The bishop addresses the whole congregation

> People of God, will you welcome *these candidates* and
> uphold *them* in *their* life in Christ?
> **With the help of God, we will.**

DECISION

A large candle may be lit. The bishop addresses all the candidates

> In baptism, God calls us out of darkness into his
> marvellous light.
> To follow Christ means dying to sin and rising to
> new life with him.
> Therefore I ask:

Do you reject the devil and all rebellion against God?
I reject them.
Do you renounce the deceit and corruption of evil?
I renounce them.
Do you repent of the sins that separate us from
    God and neighbour?
I repent of them.

Do you turn to Christ as Saviour?
I turn to Christ.
Do you submit to Christ as Lord?
I submit to Christ.
Do you come to Christ, the way, the truth and the life?
I come to Christ.

The bishop says

May God who has given you the desire to follow Christ
give you strength to continue in the Way. **Amen.**

The ministers and candidates for confirmation gather at the baptismal font. A canticle, psalm, hymn or a litany may be used.

PROFESSION OF FAITH

The bishop addresses the congregation

Brothers and sisters, I ask you to profess
together with *these candidates*
the faith of the Church.

Do you believe and trust in God the Father?
I believe in God, the Father almighty,
creator of heaven and earth.

Do you believe and trust in his Son Jesus Christ?
I believe in Jesus Christ, his only Son, our Lord,
who was conceived by the Holy Spirit,
born of the Virgin Mary,
suffered under Pontius Pilate,
was crucified, died, and was buried;
he descended to the dead.

On the third day he rose again;
he ascended into heaven,
he is seated at the right hand of the Father,
and he will come to judge the living
      and the dead.

Do you believe and trust in the Holy Spirit?
I believe in the Holy Spirit,
the holy catholic Church,
the communion of saints,
the forgiveness of sins,
the resurrection of the body,
and the life everlasting. Amen.

The candidates may come forward to the font and sign themselves with water, or the bishop may sprinkle them.

Then the bishop says
Almighty God,
we thank you for our fellowship in the household of faith
with all who have been baptized into your name.
Keep us faithful to our baptism,
and so make us ready for that day
when the whole creation shall be made perfect
      in your Son,
our Saviour Jesus Christ. **Amen.**

The bishop and the candidates gather at the place of confirmation. A hymn, chant or litany may be used.

CONFIRMATION
The bishop stands before those who are to be confirmed, and says
Our help is in the name of the Lord
who has made heaven and earth.

Blessed be the name of the Lord
now and for ever. Amen.

The bishop extends his hands towards those to be confirmed and says

Almighty and ever-living God,
you have given these your servants new birth
in baptism by water and the Spirit,
and have forgiven them all their sins.
Let your Holy Spirit rest upon them:
the Spirit of wisdom and understanding;
the Spirit of counsel and inward strength;
the Spirit of knowledge and true godliness;
and let their delight be in the fear of the Lord. **Amen.**

The bishop addresses each candidate by name

N, God has called you by name and made you his own.

He then lays his hand on the head of each, saying

Confirm, O Lord, your servant with your Holy Spirit.
Amen.

The bishop invites the congregation to pray for all those on whom hands have been laid

**Defend, O Lord, these your servants with your
    heavenly grace,
that they may continue yours for ever,
and daily increase in your Holy Spirit more and more
until they come to your everlasting kingdom. Amen.**

COMMISSION

The bishop may use this Commission

Those who are baptized are called to worship
    and serve God.
Will you continue in the apostles' teaching
    and fellowship,
in the breaking of bread, and in the prayers?
With the help of God, I will.

Will you persevere in resisting evil,
and, whenever you fall into sin, repent and return
    to the Lord?
With the help of God, I will.

Will you proclaim by word and example
the good news of God in Christ?
With the help of God, I will.

Will you seek and serve Christ in all people,
loving your neighbour as yourself?
With the help of God, I will.

Will you acknowledge Christ's authority over
    human society,
by prayer for the world and its leaders,
by defending the weak, and by seeking peace and justice?
With the help of God, I will.

May Christ dwell in your hearts through faith,
that you may be rooted and grounded in love
and bring forth the fruit of the Spirit. **Amen.**

PEACE

*The bishop introduces the Peace in these or other suitable words
(seasonal forms are provided in Appendix 2 of the service for* Holy
Baptism*)*

God has made us one in Christ.
He has set his seal upon us
and, as a pledge of what is to come,
has given the Spirit to dwell in our hearts.

The peace of the Lord be always with you.
And also with you.

> *A minister may say*
> Let us offer one another a sign of peace.
> *All may exchange a sign of peace.*

Prayers

*The service continues with suitable prayers, ending with the Lord's
Prayer. It is appropriate that the newly confirmed take their part in
leading the prayers. The prayers provided on pages 28-9 or on pages
119-21 may be used.*

Sending Out

BLESSING

The bishop may use a seasonal blessing (Appendix 2 of the service for Holy Baptism), or another suitable blessing, or

> The God of all grace,
> who called you to his eternal glory in Christ Jesus,
> establish, strengthen and settle you in the faith;
> and the blessing of God almighty,
> the Father, the Son and the Holy Spirit,
> be upon you and remain with you always. **Amen.**

DISMISSAL

> Go in the light and peace of Christ.
> **Thanks be to God.**

From Easter to Pentecost **Alleluia Alleluia** *may be added after both the versicle and response.*

The bishop may lead the newly confirmed through the church.

Affirmation of Baptismal Faith or Reception into the Communion of the Church of England
including Provision in the Absence of the Bishop

Affirmation of Baptismal Faith does not of necessity require the presence of the bishop and may be presided over by a priest. Reception into the Communion of the Church of England is governed by Canon B 28; except where the person concerned is a priest, the service may be presided over by the parish priest. The form to be followed when this is incorporated into the normal pattern of parish worship is set out opposite.

AFFIRMATION/ RECEPTION	THE EUCHARIST	MORNING OR EVENING PRAYER	A SERVICE OF THE WORD
	Omit Prayers of Penitence. The Creed or Affirmation of Faith is replaced by the Profession of Faith.	The Prayers of Penitence may be omitted. The Creed or Affirmation of Faith is replaced by the Profession of Faith.	Omit Prayers of Penitence. The Creed or Affirmation of Faith is replaced by the Profession of Faith.
PRESENTATION	Use relevant parts either before the Collect or after the Sermon	Use relevant parts after second lesson	Use relevant parts either as part of the Preparation or after the Ministry of the Word
DECISION* & PROFESSION OF FAITH [If possible, the Profession of Faith should be used near to the font]	After the Sermon	Following the Presentation	After the Ministry of the Word
AFFIRMATION OF BAPTISMAL FAITH	As applicable	As applicable	As applicable
RECEPTION INTO COMMUNION	As applicable	As applicable	As applicable
COMMISSION	Optional	Optional	Optional
PRAYERS OF INTERCESSION	Use in the Prayers	Use in the Prayers	Use in the Prayers
WELCOME & PEACE	Optional at the Peace	Optional before or after the Prayers or at the end	Optional before or after the Prayers or at the end
GIVING OF A LIGHTED CANDLE	Optional	Optional	Optional

* Where pastorally appropriate

Affirmation of Baptismal Faith at the Eucharist
including Provision in the Absence of the Bishop

Affirmation of Baptismal Faith does not of necessity require the presence of the bishop and may be presided over by a priest.

Preparation

At the entry of the ministers, a hymn may be sung.

GREETING

The president greets the people, using these or other suitable words

Blessed be God, Father, Son and Holy Spirit.
Blessed be his kingdom, now and for ever. Amen.

or from Easter Day to Pentecost
Alleluia Christ is risen.
He is risen indeed. Alleluia.

There is one body and one spirit.
There is one hope to which we were called;
one Lord, one faith, one baptism,
one God and Father of all.

The Lord be with you.
And also with you.

Gloria in Excelsis may be used.

The Presentation of the Candidates may take place here or after the Sermon.

COLLECT

The president introduces a period of silent prayer with the words
Let us pray *or a more specific bidding.*

The collect of the day is normally used on Sundays and on principal festivals. On other occasions a seasonal collect from the appendices to the service for Holy Baptism *or this prayer is used*

>Heavenly Father,
>by the power of your Holy Spirit
>you give to your faithful people new life in the
>   water of baptism.
>Guide and strengthen us by the same Spirit,
>that we who are born again may serve you in
>   faith and love,
>and grow into the full stature of your Son, Jesus Christ,
>who is alive and reigns with you in the unity of
>   the Holy Spirit
>now and for ever. **Amen.**

Liturgy of the Word

The readings of the day are normally used on Sundays and principal festivals. For other occasions a Table of Readings is provided in the Appendix.

Either one or two readings from scripture precede the gospel reading. At the end of each the reader may say

>This is the word of the Lord.
>**Thanks be to God.**

The psalm or canticle follows the first reading; other hymns and songs may be used between the readings.

GOSPEL READING

An acclamation may herald the gospel reading.

Hear the gospel of our Lord Jesus Christ according to *N*.
Glory to you, O Lord.

At the end

This is the gospel of the Lord.
Praise to you, O Christ.

SERMON

Affirmation of Baptismal Faith

PRESENTATION OF THE CANDIDATES

The candidates are presented to the congregation.

The president asks those affirming their faith

Have you been baptized in the name of the Father, and of
the Son, and of the Holy Spirit?
I have.

Are you ready with your own mouth and from your own
heart to affirm your faith in Jesus Christ?
I am.

Testimony by the candidates may follow.

The president addresses the whole congregation

People of God, will you [welcome *these candidates* and]
    uphold *them* in *their* life in Christ?
With the help of God, we will.

DECISION*

A large candle may be lit. The president addresses all the candidates

In baptism, God calls us out of darkness into his
    marvellous light.
To follow Christ means dying to sin and rising to
    new life with him.
Therefore I ask:

Do you reject the devil and all rebellion against God?
I reject them.
Do you renounce the deceit and corruption of evil?
I renounce them.
Do you repent of the sins that separate us from
    God and neighbour?
I repent of them.

Do you turn to Christ as Saviour?
I turn to Christ.
Do you submit to Christ as Lord?
I submit to Christ.
Do you come to Christ, the way, the truth
    and the life?
I come to Christ.

The president may say

May God who has given you the desire to follow Christ
give you strength to continue in the Way. **Amen.**

*The ministers and those who are to affirm their baptismal faith gather
at the baptismal font. A canticle, psalm, hymn or a litany may be
used.*

PROFESSION OF FAITH

The president addresses the congregation

Brothers and sisters, I ask you to profess
together with *these candidates*
the faith of the Church.

Do you believe and trust in God the Father?
**I believe in God, the Father almighty,
creator of heaven and earth.**

* *If pastorally appropriate*

Do you believe and trust in his Son Jesus Christ?
I believe in Jesus Christ, his only Son, our Lord,
who was conceived by the Holy Spirit,
born of the Virgin Mary,
suffered under Pontius Pilate,
was crucified, died, and was buried;
he descended to the dead.
On the third day he rose again;
he ascended into heaven,
he is seated at the right hand of the Father,
and he will come to judge the living
and the dead.

Do you believe and trust in the Holy Spirit?
I believe in the Holy Spirit,
the holy catholic Church,
the communion of saints,
the forgiveness of sins,
the resurrection of the body,
and the life everlasting. Amen.

DECLARATION

Those who are to affirm their baptismal faith stand before the president, who says

I call upon those who are affirming their baptismal faith
to renew their commitment to Jesus Christ.

The candidates face the people and make this declaration

I answer the call of God my creator.
I trust in Jesus Christ as my Saviour.
I seek new life from the Holy Spirit.

The congregation responds

God, who has called you, is faithful.
Rejoice in your baptism into Jesus Christ.
Walk with us in the life of the Spirit.

The candidates may come forward to the font and sign themselves with water, or the president may sprinkle them.

Then the president says

Almighty God,
we thank you for our fellowship in the household of faith
with all who have been baptized into your name.
Keep us faithful to our baptism,
and so make us ready for that day
when the whole creation shall be made perfect
in your Son,
our Saviour Jesus Christ. **Amen.**

The president and the candidates gather before the congregation. A hymn, chant or litany may be used.

AFFIRMATION OF BAPTISMAL FAITH

The president extends his/her hands towards those who seek to affirm their baptismal faith and says

God of mercy and love,
in baptism you welcome the sinner
and restore the dead to life.
You create a clean heart in those who repent,
and give your Holy Spirit to those who ask.
Grant that these your servants may grow
into the fullness of the stature of Christ.
Equip them with the gifts of your Holy Spirit,
and fill them with faith in Jesus Christ
and with love for all your people,
in the service of your kingdom. **Amen.**

The president lays his/her hand on each one, saying

N, may God renew his life within you
that you may confess his name this day and for ever.
Amen.

> **Defend, O Lord, these your servants with your**
> **heavenly grace,**
> **that they may continue yours for ever,**
> **and daily increase in your Holy Spirit more and more**
> **until they come to your everlasting kingdom. Amen.**

COMMISSION

The president may use this Commission

> Those who are baptized are called to worship
> and serve God.

> Will you continue in the apostles' teaching
> and fellowship,
> in the breaking of bread, and in the prayers?
> **With the help of God, I will.**

> Will you persevere in resisting evil,
> and, whenever you fall into sin, repent and return
> to the Lord?
> **With the help of God, I will.**

> Will you proclaim by word and example
> the good news of God in Christ?
> **With the help of God, I will.**

> Will you seek and serve Christ in all people,
> loving your neighbour as yourself?
> **With the help of God, I will.**

> Will you acknowledge Christ's authority over
> human society,
> by prayer for the world and its leaders,
> by defending the weak, and by seeking peace and justice?
> **With the help of God, I will.**

> May Christ dwell in your hearts through faith,
> that you may be rooted and grounded in love
> and bring forth the fruit of the Spirit. **Amen.**

The Prayers of Intercession may follow. The prayers provided on pages 28-9 may be used.

PEACE

The president introduces the Peace in these or other suitable words (seasonal forms are provided in Appendix 2 of the service for Holy Baptism)

> God has made us one in Christ.
> He has set his seal upon us
> and, as a pledge of what is to come,
> has given the Spirit to dwell in our hearts.
>
> The peace of the Lord be always with you.
> **And also with you.**

A minister may say

> Let us offer one another a sign of peace.

All may exchange a sign of peace.

If the Liturgy of the Eucharist does not follow immediately, the service continues with suitable prayers, ending with the Lord's Prayer and the Sending Out. One or more of the prayers on pages 120-1 may be used.

Liturgy of the Eucharist

The Eucharist continues with

PREPARATION OF THE TABLE

TAKING OF THE BREAD AND WINE

EUCHARISTIC PRAYER

This proper preface may be used

> And now we give you thanks,
> because by water and the Holy Spirit
> you have made us a holy people in Jesus Christ our Lord;
> you raise us to new life in him
> and renew in us the image of your glory.

LORD'S PRAYER

BREAKING OF THE BREAD

GIVING OF THE BREAD AND WINE

PRAYER AFTER COMMUNION

The authorized post communion prayer for the day is normally used on Sundays and on principal festivals. On other occasions a seasonal prayer from Appendix 2 of the service for Holy Baptism *or this prayer is used*

> God of mercy,
> by whose grace alone we are accepted
> and equipped for your service:
> stir up in us the gifts of your Holy Spirit
> and make us worthy of our calling;
> that we may bring forth the fruit of the Spirit
> in love and joy and peace;
> through Jesus Christ our Lord. **Amen.**

Sending Out

BLESSING

The president may use a seasonal blessing (Appendix 2 of the service for Holy Baptism*), or another suitable blessing, or*

> The God of all grace,
> who called you to his eternal glory in Christ Jesus,
> establish, strengthen and settle you in the faith;
> and the blessing of God almighty,
> the Father, the Son and the Holy Spirit,
> be upon you and remain with you always. **Amen.**

DISMISSAL

> Go in the light and peace of Christ.
> **Thanks be to God.**

From Easter to Pentecost **Alleluia Alleluia** *may be added after both the versicle and response.*

Reception into the Communion of the Church of England at the Eucharist
including Provision in the Absence of the Bishop

Reception into the Communion of the Church of England is governed by Canon B 28; except where the person concerned is a priest, the service may be presided over by the parish priest.

Preparation

At the entry of the ministers, a hymn may be sung.

GREETING
The president greets the people, using these or other suitable words

Blessed be God, Father, Son and Holy Spirit.
Blessed be his kingdom, now and for ever. Amen.

or from Easter Day to Pentecost

Alleluia Christ is risen.
He is risen indeed. Alleluia.

There is one body and one spirit.
There is one hope to which we were called;
one Lord, one faith, one baptism,
one God and Father of all.

The Lord be with you.
And also with you.

Gloria in Excelsis may be used.

The Presentation of the Candidates may take place here or after the Sermon.

COLLECT

The president introduces a period of silent prayer with the words
Let us pray *or a more specific bidding.*

The collect of the day is normally used on Sundays and on principal festivals. On other occasions a seasonal collect from the appendices to the service for Holy Baptism *or this prayer is used*

> Heavenly Father,
> by the power of your Holy Spirit
> you give your faithful people new life in the
>   water of baptism.
> Guide and strengthen us by the same Spirit,
> that we who are born again may serve you in
>   faith and love,
> and grow into the full stature of your Son, Jesus Christ,
> who is alive and reigns with you in the unity of
>   the Holy Spirit
> now and for ever. **Amen.**

Liturgy of the Word

The readings of the day are normally used on Sundays and principal festivals. For other occasions a Table of Readings is provided in the Appendix.

Either one or two readings from scripture precede the gospel reading. At the end of each the reader may say

> This is the word of the Lord.
> **Thanks be to God.**

The psalm or canticle follows the first reading; other hymns and songs may be used between the readings.

GOSPEL READING

An acclamation may herald the gospel reading.

When the gospel is announced the reader says

Hear the gospel of our Lord Jesus Christ according to *N.*
Glory to you, O Lord.

At the end

This is the gospel of the Lord.
Praise to you, O Christ.

SERMON

Reception into the Communion of the Church of England

PRESENTATION OF THE CANDIDATES

The candidates are presented to the congregation.

The president asks the candidates

Have you been baptized in the name of the Father, and of the Son, and of the Holy Spirit?
I have.

Are you ready with your own mouth and from your own heart to affirm your faith in Jesus Christ?
I am.

DECISION*

A large candle may be lit. The president addresses all the candidates

In baptism, God calls us out of darkness into his marvellous light.
To follow Christ means dying to sin and rising to new life with him.
Therefore I ask:

* If pastorally appropriate

Do you reject the devil and all rebellion against God?
I reject them.
Do you renounce the deceit and corruption of evil?
I renounce them.
Do you repent of the sins that separate us from
    God and neighbour?
I repent of them.

Do you turn to Christ as Saviour?
I turn to Christ.
Do you submit to Christ as Lord?
I submit to Christ.
Do you come to Christ, the way, the truth
    and the life?
I come to Christ.

The president may say

May God who has given you the desire to follow Christ
give you strength to continue in the Way. **Amen.**

*The ministers and candidates for reception into the communion of the
Church of England gather at the baptismal font. A canticle, psalm,
hymn or a litany may be used.*

PROFESSION OF FAITH

The president addresses the congregation

Brothers and sisters, I ask you to profess
together with *these candidates*
the faith of the Church.

Do you believe and trust in God the Father?
**I believe in God, the Father almighty,
creator of heaven and earth.**

Do you believe and trust in his Son Jesus Christ?
**I believe in Jesus Christ, his only Son, our Lord,
who was conceived by the Holy Spirit,
born of the Virgin Mary,
suffered under Pontius Pilate,
was crucified, died, and was buried;
he descended to the dead.**

On the third day he rose again;
he ascended into heaven,
he is seated at the right hand of the Father,
and he will come to judge the living
    and the dead.

Do you believe and trust in the Holy Spirit?
I believe in the Holy Spirit,
the holy catholic Church,
the communion of saints,
the forgiveness of sins,
the resurrection of the body,
and the life everlasting. Amen.

DECLARATION

Those who are to be received into the communion of the Church of England stand before the president to make this declaration.

The president says

You are here to be received into the communion of the Church of England.

Do you acknowledge the Church of England as part of the one, holy, catholic and apostolic Church?
I do.

Do you accept the teaching, discipline and authority of the Church of England?
I do.

Will you take part with us in worship and mission?
I will.

The candidates seeking reception may come forward to the font and sign themselves with water, or the president may sprinkle them.

Then the president says

Almighty God,
we thank you for our fellowship in the household of faith
with all who have been baptized into your name.
Keep us faithful to our baptism,
and so make us ready for that day
when the whole creation shall be made perfect
    in your Son,
our Saviour Jesus Christ. **Amen.**

*The president and the candidates gather before the congregation. A
hymn, chant or litany may be used.*

RECEPTION INTO THE COMMUNION
OF THE CHURCH OF ENGLAND

*The president extends his/her hands towards those who are to be
received and says*

God of mercy and love,
by one Spirit we have all been baptized into one body
and made to drink of the one Spirit;
we thank you for the gifts you have given to these
    your servants
for the building up of the body of Christ.
Grant that they may continue in the life of the Spirit
and walk with us in the light and obedience of Christ.
By the same Spirit, fill the whole Church
with your overflowing love;
give us knowledge and discernment of your will,
and steadfastness in your service,
until we all come to the unity of the faith,
to the measure of the full stature of Christ,
through whom we make our prayer. **Amen.**

The president takes the hand of each person to be received, saying

N, we recognize you as a member of the one, holy,
   catholic and apostolic Church;
and we receive you into the communion of the
   Church of England
in the name of the Father, and of the Son, and of
   the Holy Spirit. **Amen.**

*The president invites the congregation to pray for those received into
the communion of the Church of England*

**Defend, O Lord, these your servants with your
   heavenly grace,
that they may continue yours for ever,
and daily increase in your Holy Spirit more and more
until they come to your everlasting kingdom. Amen.**

COMMISSION

The president may use this Commission

Those who are baptized are called to worship and
   serve God.

Will you continue in the apostles' teaching
   and fellowship,
in the breaking of bread, and in the prayers?
With the help of God, I will.

Will you persevere in resisting evil,
and, whenever you fall into sin, repent and return
   to the Lord?
With the help of God, I will.

Will you proclaim by word and example
the good news of God in Christ?
With the help of God, I will.

Will you seek and serve Christ in all people,
loving your neighbour as yourself?
With the help of God, I will.

Will you acknowledge Christ's authority over
    human society,
by prayer for the world and its leaders,
by defending the weak, and by seeking peace and justice?
With the help of God, I will.

May Christ dwell in your hearts through faith,
that you may be rooted and grounded in love
and bring forth the fruit of the Spirit. **Amen.**

*The Prayers of Intercession may follow. The prayers provided on pages
28-9 may be used.*

PEACE

*The president introduces the Peace in these or other suitable words
(seasonal forms are provided in Appendix 2 of the service for* Holy
Baptism*)*

God has made us one in Christ.
He has set his seal upon us
and, as a pledge of what is to come,
has given the Spirit to dwell in our hearts.

The peace of the Lord be always with you.
And also with you.

A minister may say

Let us offer one another a sign of peace.

All may exchange a sign of peace.

*If the Liturgy of the Eucharist does not follow immediately, the service
continues with suitable prayers, ending with the Lord's Prayer and the
Sending Out. One or more of the prayers on pages 120-1 may be
used.*

Liturgy of the Eucharist

The Eucharist continues with

PREPARATION OF THE TABLE

TAKING OF THE BREAD AND WINE

EUCHARISTIC PRAYER

This proper preface may be used

> And now we give you thanks,
> because by water and the Holy Spirit
> you have made us a holy people in Jesus Christ our Lord;
> you raise us to new life in him
> and renew in us the image of your glory.

LORD'S PRAYER

BREAKING OF THE BREAD

GIVING OF THE BREAD AND WINE

PRAYER AFTER COMMUNION

The authorized post communion prayer for the day is normally used on Sundays and on principal festivals. On other occasions a seasonal prayer from Appendix 2 of the service for Holy Baptism *or this prayer is used*

> God of mercy,
> by whose grace alone we are accepted
> and equipped for your service:
> stir up in us the gifts of your Holy Spirit
> and make us worthy of our calling;
> that we may bring forth the fruit of the Spirit
> in love and joy and peace;
> through Jesus Christ our Lord. **Amen.**

Sending Out

BLESSING

The president may use a seasonal blessing (Appendix 2 of the service for Holy Baptism*), or another suitable blessing, or*

> The God of all grace,
> who called you to his eternal glory in Christ Jesus,
> establish, strengthen and settle you in the faith;
> and the blessing of God almighty,
> the Father, the Son and the Holy Spirit,
> be upon you and remain with you always. **Amen.**

DISMISSAL

> Go in the light and peace of Christ.
> **Thanks be to God.**

From Easter to Pentecost **Alleluia Alleluia** *may be added after both the versicle and response.*

Appendix

Bible Readings and Psalms at Confirmation

Sets of readings follow grouped under the headings:
> General
> Epiphany/Baptism of Christ/Trinity
> Easter/Pentecost
> All Saints

Two sets are provided under each heading for use
  a at Confirmation
  b when Affirmation or Reception take place, for which they are
     particularly suitable

	OLD TESTAMENT	PSALM	NEW TESTAMENT	GOSPEL
1	**General**			
a	Ezekiel 36.24-28	Psalm 51.6-13	Titus 3.3-7	John 3.1-8
	or Ezekiel 47.1-10,12	Psalm 84.1-7	1 Corinthians 12.4 -13	John 7.37-39
b	Isaiah 44.1-5	Psalm 18.30-37	Ephesians 6.10-20	Luke 24.44-49
	or Isaiah 62.1-7	Psalm 107.1-9	Acts 10.34-43	Luke 4.14-19
2	**Epiphany/Baptism of Christ/Trinity**			
a	Isaiah 63.7–10,17; 64.1-4	Psalm 27.1-8	1 Corinthians 2.7-12	Mark 1.4-11 (or 1-13)
b	Exodus 33.12-20	Psalm 36.5-9	2 Corinthians 3.12 – 4.6	John 1.14-18
3	**Easter/Pentecost**			
a	Ezekiel 37.1-14	Psalm 118.19-24 or Isaiah 12.2-6	Romans 8.1-11 (or 4-11)	John 20.19-23
b	Jeremiah 31.31-34	Psalm 119.105-112 or 104.27-30	Galatians 5.22 – 6.2 or Acts 2.1-18	John 14.15-18 John 4.23-26
4	**All Saints**			
a	Isaiah 11.1-10	Psalm 20.6-9	Revelation 5.6-10	Matthew 28.16-20
b	Exodus 19.3-8	Psalm 96.1-10	1 Peter 2.4-10	Mark 1.14-20

Commentary by the Liturgical Commission

This Commentary draws on the Report to the House of Bishops, On The Way: Towards an Integrated Approach to Christian Initiation *(Church House Publishing 1995) as well as reports of the Liturgical Commission and the General Synod's Revision Committee on the Initiation Services.*

Background

The rediscovery of baptism

Over the last hundred years Christians have been involved in the rediscovery of the meaning of baptism. Before this, baptism was generally treated as a sort of birth rite within a Christian society. Where there was controversy it often reflected other anxieties – such as the nature of salvation, the importance of personal faith, or a desire to clarify the boundaries of the Church in a more sceptical culture – rather than an appreciation of the theological importance of baptism itself. Various factors have contributed to a revival of baptismal theology: overseas mission, patristic and biblical study, the changing social context of the Church.

The World Council of Churches' 1982 Lima Document, *Baptism, Eucharist and Ministry*, shows that baptism continues to be an area of controversy and division, but provides eloquent testimony to the theological richness that the churches are now finding in this sacrament. There was a tendency to see baptism as an isolated moment in the Christian life and as the gateway to the eucharist, itself the one proper sacramental focus of the Christian life. Increasingly baptism is seen as a sacrament of significance in its own right that points Christians to their true identity, character and calling. Paul repeatedly refers his hearers back to baptism not simply as a reminder of their conversion but as a way of bringing home to them what it is to be in Christ.[1]

Towards an integrated approach to Christian initiation

The report *On The Way* identifies the need to reintegrate baptismal practice both with a congregation's commitment to the mission of God in the world and with the individual candidate's journey to faith and his or her primary formation in the Christian life. It proposes the following framework as a check list against which the Church can evaluate its approach to Christian initiation.

FIVE ELEMENTS OF CHRISTIAN INITIATION

1 CHURCH Initiation calls the Church:
- to see itself as a baptized people
- to welcome and learn from the enquirer
- to be active in mission and service
- to expect the anointing of the Holy Spirit
- to walk with those seeking faith
- to stand with the despised and oppressed
- to look for the unity of God's people

2 WELCOME Enquirers need a welcome:
- that is personal
- that is public
- that accepts their starting point
- that expects the presence of God in their lives
- that is willing to travel with them at their pace

3 PRAYER Initiation involves prayer:
- for enquirer and Church
- to discern the presence of God
- to open up to the grace of God
- to support the process of change
- to discover the moments of decision
- to receive and recognize the gifts of God

4 THE WAY Discipleship means learning:
- to worship with the Church
- to grow in prayer
- to listen to the scriptures
- to serve our neighbour

5 GOAL The goal of initiation is:
- relationship with God the Holy Trinity
- life and worship with the Church
- service and witness in the world

---

[1] *On The Way 4.41/4.42*

On The Way also proposed that four basic texts should be adopted as integral to an individual's personal formation: the Lord's Prayer, the Apostles' Creed, the Summary of the Law and the Beatitudes.

The ministry of the bishop in initiation

In an episcopally ordered church the bishop is the chief minister of the whole process of Christian initiation and is integral to its practice. This finds expression in a number of features of current practice: the requirement of episcopal confirmation (Canon B 27; B 15A); the canonical requirement that the bishop be given notice of an adult baptism (Canon B 24.2); the final say resting with the bishop over a refusal to baptize an infant (Canon B 22.2), and over any attempt to bar a baptized person from receiving communion (Canon B 16).[2]

The bishop is charged with focusing the mission and unity of the Church: as such he has a particular responsibility to keep the way open for enquirers, to oversee their proper formation in the Christian way, and to ensure that they take their rightful place within the wider fellowship of the Church. The purpose of the bishop's ministry in initiation is to enable the whole process so that the journey of those coming to faith is protected and affirmed. The focus of initiation is not the needs of the Church or the bishop; it is about the joyful entry into full Christian life of the person coming to faith.[3]

The bishop's role requires the bishop, either himself or through others, to guide the Church in initiation:

- in focusing the mission and unity of the Church
- in teaching the faith
- in protecting and providing for the enquirer
- in affirming and praying for those coming to faith
- in recognizing the decision of faith

Parish policies on initiation

Parishes and congregations need to have a clear and developing grasp of their approach to initiation. This implies the involvement of the PCC (or equivalent) and wider church fellowship, not simply an initiative by the clergy. What is more, such parish policies and approaches must have regard for those particular concerns which are embodied in the bishop's oversight of initiation. This means that each parish would need to identify and own its approach to the welcome and formation of new believers. These approaches should be worked out in appropriate dialogue with the bishop and should cover:

- the welcome, formation and sacramental initiation of adult enquirers

- an appropriate pattern for responding to requests by non-churchgoing parents for their children's baptism

---

[2] *OTW 7.5* [3] *OTW 7.7*

- an appropriate pattern for the admission to communion of children baptized in infancy

- provision (where appropriate) marking the entry into adulthood of young people growing up within the Church.[4]

Story, journey and the Way

In Acts 9.1-31 Paul's conversion is not complete with the dramatic religious experience described in verses 3-9. It reaches its conclusion with verse 19, after the church in Damascus has played its part in the welcome and incorporation of the new believer. The figure of Ananias and the unnamed disciples of verse 19 are integral to the story. The flow of the narrative includes five elements without which Paul's initiation would have been defective: welcome, spiritual discernment, prayer, baptism, and incorporation into the community of the church.

The passage also indicates the importance of stories and story telling in Christian experience and therefore in Christian initiation. The story of Paul's conversion is told three times in Acts. Christian initiation cannot be reduced to doctrinal and moral instruction or liturgical rites; it must include the narrative of rounded human experience. Christian formation must allow an individual's story to be heard and to find its place within the unfolding story of faith in the Church and in the scriptures. There must be appropriate space in the processes surrounding baptism for the telling and retelling of human stories.

It is while Paul is on the road that he meets the risen Christ. Journey is a major image in the narrative of scripture from the call of Abraham through to the itinerant ministry of Jesus and beyond. As an image of human life and of the passage to faith it allows both for the integration of faith and human experience and also for the necessity of change and development.[5]

In this story of Paul's conversion the first Christians were known as the Way (Acts 9.2 cf. 18.25,26; 19.9,23; 22.4; 24.14,22). As a name for life in the Christian church, the term Way draws together three important dimensions of Christian discipleship: movement, integration and pattern. This last provides an important complement to the open-endedness of the idea of journey. Much New Testament church life and instruction was about establishing appropriate patterns in the believing and living of Christian communities and individuals. In the New Testament the Greek word *tupos* (pattern, example, imprint) points to this important dimension of Christian formation (cf Romans 6.17; Philippians 3.17; 1 Timothy 1.16; 4.12; 2 Timothy 1.13; Titus 2.7). The idea of communicating a shape to Christian gathering, believing and living occurs much more widely than the term itself. Satisfactory approaches to Christian initiation need to reflect the dimensions of open-endedness, integration and patterning that are present in the idea of the Way.[6]

---

[4] *OTW 8.2* [5] *OTW 2.2* [6] *OTW 2.3*

A theological framework

In preparing these services and additional supporting rites the Liturgical Commission had before it the following biblical framework, believing that baptism involves:

- **separation** from this world – that is, the world alienated from God, and

- **reception** into a universal community centred on God, within which

- his children can **grow** into the fullness of the pattern of Christ, and

- a community whose **mission** is to serve God's Spirit in redeeming the world.

Separation. The 'world' in the New Testament sense fails to 'give God glory' (Romans 1.21) and is thus subject to forces other than God, a condition manifest in idolatry. This social blindness and estrangement is the root sin of which actual sins are symptoms. Sin and righteousness are primarily terms of relationship from which corresponding attitudes and acts derive.

Reception. The root remedy for sin is therefore the creating of relationship in a community centred on God with a new pattern of life. For their right growth new human beings need to be grafted in from the start.

This separation and reception are expressed in the New Testament by a rich variety of overlapping metaphors. In these metaphors God's action is primary; so, for example, repentance (change of heart and direction) is seen not as human achievement (Jeremiah 13.23) but as response to God's gracious initiative. Images of drastic change can be taken as picturing a moment or event and are complemented by the journey motif. Exodus leads on to Sinai and the giving of a new covenant and torah; Easter is followed by Pentecost and the Holy Spirit as God's law internalized as promised by Jeremiah (31.31-4); the Church as the Israel of God, his army marching to the promised land through the desert of testing, but with guidance and provision for the journey (1 Corinthians 10.1-13), and with spiritual armour for Christ's soldiers and servants (Ephesians 6.10-18; 2 Timothy 2.3-5,15).

Growth and transformation. Thus reception into the community is the beginning of a journey of growth into the pattern of Christ, learning obedience through testing and temptation, just as Jesus' baptism was followed by a period of adjustment and testing (cf Hebrews 5.8,9). This journey will pass through different stages of maturity and responsibility; there will be crises, reversals and renewals which it may sometimes be appropriate to acknowledge and support in a public way.

Mission. God's purpose in bringing members of the community to full growth (the stature of Christ, Ephesians 4.13) is through them to establish his rule over the world ('the kingdom of God') and bring the world to perfection. The goal can be seen both as this-worldly and social ('a new heaven and a new earth') with responsibility for the social order, and as other-worldly and individual, entry into the life of the world to come, of which the Holy Spirit is foretaste and pledge (Romans 8.23; 2 Corinthians 1.22; Hebrews 6.5). This is what the Greek Fathers called sharing in the divine nature (2 Peter 1.4; cf 2 Corinthians 8.9), and Irenaeus expresses as 'he became man that we might become God', a process which begins at baptism. Baptism can thus be seen as the beginning (Greek *arche*), which holds within itself its goal (Greek *telos*), as already given but not yet worked out. This may help to see how 'moment' includes within itself 'process', and points beyond space-time to the eternal, the resurrection reality which is in time and beyond it. It also shows how entry into the new community is also entry into the life of the Trinity, putting on Christ who in his baptism was acknowledged as Son by the Father and indwelt by the Spirit.

This baptismal framework is communicated in scripture through a rich tapestry of imagery. Some images cover part of the process; others provide an interpretative picture for the whole. All have a claim to be reflected within any liturgy of baptism; some need to be highlighted either in the preparation for baptism or in reflection after the celebration of baptism.

Church context

(See the table on the opposite page.) In framing one basic liturgy for the baptism of both infants and those who can answer for themselves, the Church is declaring that:

- God's prevenient grace is central (Romans 5.6-8). Baptism is seen as acted evangelism, proclaiming in Christ's death and resurrection God's victory over the world powers of chaos and darkness to establish the new creation.

- A renewed and Christ-centred understanding of covenant is important. Baptism is the outward sign and ritual mark of incorporation into the people of the New Covenant, sealed by Christ's death. God gives the covenant (Exodus 19.3-6; Jeremiah 31.31-4; 1 Corinthians 11.25; 2 Corinthians 3.6); it carries unfolding obligations, but these are the response to God's grace, made possible by his Spirit.

- There is a social aspect of baptism alongside the purely individual. Baptism establishes a corporate belonging, delineating the new world and community and the radical difference between the old and the new. This points to a strengthening of the baptismal affirmations and renunciations. (There is an interesting example from the proposed Ecumenical Baptismal Liturgy of Sri Lanka: 'Do you renounce being ruled by the desires of this world, the flesh and Satan, particularly the snare of pride, the love and worship of money, the power of violence?')

- The liturgy of baptism needs to recognize that coming to faith in Christ involves a personal and social process (what the Toronto Statement calls the 'catechumenal process'[7]). This is spelt out in *On The Way*: pre-baptismal preparation both for candidates and their families and for the community into which they will be baptized; continuing post-baptismal formation, opening hearts and minds to the pattern centred on Christ crucified, a reversal of this world's ideas and values; and rites to mark stages on the way, so that they may be appropriated within the community. Infant baptism is open to objection if this process is not clearly signalled (cf *On The Way* 5.38).

[7] *Walk in the Newness of Life 2.14.2*

liberation	liberation	Exodus
		1 Corinthians 10.1-4
	rescue from the power of darkness and sin	Colossians 1.12-14
		Revelation 1.5
new creation	new creation	Galatians 6.15
		2 Corinthians 5.17
		Isaiah 51.9-11
	liberation from Babylon as a new exodus, defeating the dragon of chaos	Genesis 1.2
new birth	'from above'	John 3.3ff
		1 Peter 1.12
		James 1.18
reconciliation	removal of enmity	Romans 5.6-11
		2 Corinthians 5.18 – 6.2
illumination	illumination	2 Corinthians 4.4-6
		Genesis 1.3
	opening of eyes, ears, hearts and minds	Ephesians 1.18
		Hebrews 6.4
		John 9
recognition	receiving the name of Christ	James 2.7
		Isaiah 43.1
cleansing	washing	Ephesians 5.26
		Hebrews 10.22
		Titus 3.5
	removal of defilement	Romans 3.25
		1 John 2.2; 4.10
stripping	putting off the old human the Christian analogue to circumcision	Colossians 3.9
		Colossians 2.11
clothing	putting on Christ the new human	Galatians 3.27
		Colossians 3.10
dying	drowning, burial	Romans 6.3ff
		Colossians 2.11
	participation in Christ's 'exodus'	Luke 9.31
	the ordeal foreshadowed in his own baptism	Luke 12.50
		Mark 10.38
resurrection	into newness of life	Romans 6.4ff
		Colossians 2;12; 3.1ff
building	as living stones into a new temple /community	1 Corinthians 3.9ff
		Ephesians 2.19-21
		1 Peter 2.4ff

Other elements of Christian life follow on from baptism. Growth and mission both require catechesis: induction into the whole of Christian living – worship, prayer, doctrine, ethics, witness and service. In the pattern inherited from the sixteenth century this has normally been expressed by baptism, then a period of instruction leading to confirmation with preparation for Holy Communion and for ministry as part of the royal priesthood. Recent years have seen the emergence of other patterns and the acceptance of a measure of diversity, as discussed in *On The Way* (pp. 64,81-3,90-6).

Whatever the pattern followed, the equipping of God's people for the work of ministry (Ephesians 4.12) will require continuing 'ministerial education' for all. This will bring ongoing discovery of what was done in baptism and of the new identity, and lead to continual putting on Christ and taking up the cross – learning to see weakness, suffering and failure as the place of redemption, glory and victory. It will welcome the new stages on the journey as the unfolding of God's baptismal covenant and promise. Some of these stages need distinct recognition beyond confirmation and Holy Communion, for example:

- **reconciliation** (confession, penance) in case of straying or fall

- **affirmation of baptismal faith** in case of lapse, or more importantly, fresh experience and commitment

- **healing** if inhibited by weakness of mind, body or will

- **deliverance** if enslaved by habit, addiction or 'evil spirits'

- **preparation for death**, at the end of one's personal journey, with death seen as the completion of dying with Christ to 'this world'.

The services have been drafted to take account of the fluid understanding of confirmation in the Anglican Communion and the different practices prevailing in the Church of England about the admission of children to communion. In particular they should not need Synodical amendment to allow for: the admission to communion of unconfirmed children; the recognition as communicant members of the Church of England, without episcopal confirmation, of members of the Nordic Churches who have received presbyteral confirmation (cf Appendix 4 of *On The Way*); and the removal, as some are urging, of the requirement of episcopal confirmation for those baptized as adults.

About the Services

These services are influenced by older traditions reflected in the *Book of Common Prayer* as well as by continued thinking in the Church that wishes to place baptism at the heart of Christian life and mission.

One baptism service for adults and infants

A single service makes clear that there is only one baptism which brings people into relationship with Christ and his Church. 'One Lord, one faith, one baptism' (Ephesians 4.5). This emphasis on one baptism has been a theme of the modern rediscovery of baptism; for example, the International Anglican Liturgical Consultation at Toronto in 1991 stated, 'The same rite, with only a minimum of adaptation, should be used for both those able and unable to answer for themselves' (4.4).

The very different personal circumstances of candidates for baptism could easily give the impression that the baptism of children and adults are fundamentally different realities. This might lead people to view the baptism of infants as less than baptism or, conversely, to regard the baptism of adults as some sort of strange aberration. For both infants and adults the service has the same inner logic, a movement from welcome and renunciation through to an identification with the people of God in their dependence on God, their profession of the saving name, and the common activities of prayer, eucharist and mission. The different life circumstances of the newly baptized finds expression in the very different form that the Commission takes in each case.

Accessible language

The full and rich biblical imagery surrounding baptism and the comparative ignorance of this richness in many sections of modern society pose a major problem in the drafting of services of Christian initiation. If this tension is resolved by having two rites, one 'churchy' and one 'simple', then the Church's witness to the unity of baptism is undermined. Another common way of resolving this difficulty has been to select one biblical image, commonly that of death and resurrection, and play down other major scriptural emphases. In particular, this has meant the marginalization of many important themes associated with the baptism of Christ that are taken up in the New Testament in the feast of Pentecost: the kingdom of God, identification with the passion of Christ, coming of the Holy Spirit, incorporation into the life of the Trinity and the mission of God in the world.

If the baptismal liturgy of the Church is to do justice to scripture it cannot be satisfactory simply to thin down the resonance to what can be absorbed at one sitting by those unfamiliar with the many themes associated with baptism. Part of the solution must lie with new approaches to preparation and more vivid presentation of the service. In framing these services a sharp distinction has been drawn between, on the one hand, the language and phrasing that could reasonably be put into the mouth of parents, godparents, sponsors and congregation and, on the other, a richer use of biblical types and allusions in presidential texts. Some would also argue that the risk of losing people by esoteric language needs to be balanced by the danger of patronizing them by simplistic wording.

Creed or Profession of Faith

In the baptism service the creed is a congregational statement of the Church's collective belief rather than a test for the candidate. Candidates are asked to join in a congregational recitation rather than making such a full statement on their own, thereby demonstrating that they are joining, and being drawn into, a community of faith.

The caution in the rubric about only using the shorter credal affirmation (Appendix 7) when there are 'strong pastoral reasons' arises from a respect for the Anglican position that the Apostles' Creed is 'the baptismal symbol' or profession (Lambeth Quadrilateral 1888). It is also important to avoid any impression of 'first' and 'second' class baptism, or any suggestion that some baptisms require a greater degree of commitment than others.

However, the view was taken that there are pastoral circumstances where a shorter credal affirmation is justified on grounds of the time, setting of the baptism and the capacity and circumstances of particular candidates, rather than as a general policy of allowing a 'lighter' option. This is not a straightforward demarcation between infants and adults; there are adults for whom a shorter affirmation might be more suitable. The form in Appendix 7 attempts to meet the criticism that the shorter creed in the ASB improperly divides the work of creation, redemption and sanctification among the separate persons of the Trinity.

The text of the Apostles' Creed used in the service is a revised version of the modern internationally agreed ecumenical text. This was made available to its member churches by the English Language Liturgical Consultation in 1988. At a number of points the revised text sticks more closely to the original Latin than the text used in the ASB. At one point the Church of England decided not to follow the international text: where this reads in line 3 'God's only Son' the Church of England has continued with the more traditional 'his only Son' on the grounds that the reference here is to the relationship between persons of the Trinity.

The use of oil and understandings of confirmation

The liturgical use of oil should be seen as part of the prayer which is integral to baptism. It is through prayer that the people of God ask for the fullness of God's blessing on the candidate and also express the dependence of the whole baptized company on the once-for-all act of God in Christ. The wealth of imagery which the scriptures use to describe this salvation is traditionally focused in the Prayer over the Water as well as in prayer for the candidate during the extended preparation and process of baptism. The particularities of such prayer have varied greatly in the practice of the Church and have often included the use of gesture and symbol. In addition the relationship of such prayer to the whole process of baptism has been articulated in different ways. Common gestures have included laying on of hands and the use of oil.

Each rite is prefaced by a Note allowing for the use of oil and indicating customary places for its use. These notes briefly refer to long-standing tradition concerning the use of pure olive oil and oil scented with fragrant spices. The use of oil in Christian initiation is practised in various traditions of the Church. It is allowed for in the ASB, and the 'blessing of oils' is a common feature in the Maundy Thursday services of many dioceses. However, others see no place for the use of additional or supplementary symbolism in the practice of baptism. This was the view taken at the Reformation when all use of oil was abolished; some would still wish to hold to that position. These different views and practices properly exist within the Church of England and imply no change in doctrine or discipline.

The practice of using oil in association with the rite of baptism has its origin in the natural use of olive oil in Mediterranean culture and draws on rich scriptural imagery. The outward application of oil to the body had a number of distinct uses: healing; cleansing and as a sign of celebration. Oil was used for healing and to prepare an athlete's body for the contest. It was associated with washing and was used to cleanse, soften and protect the body. Again it functioned as a sign of blessing, empowerment and joy. The increasing use of oils for cosmetic or healing purposes in modern culture marks an interesting point of contact with older practice. These practices in biblical cultures provide the background for the use of oil in the anointing of prophets, priests and kings. Theologically one of its most important uses, the anointing of a king, gives us the title Christ (Messiah), the anointed one. Oil made fragrant with spices (often called chrism) has therefore been used in a variety of Christian traditions as a sign of participation in the community of the Anointed One and in the royal priesthood of the Church.

In the historic Western tradition pure olive oil has been used before baptism as part of the preparation of the Christian athlete for the struggle of faith. Similarly chrism has been used in rites that follow baptism as a sign of the blessings brought by the Holy Spirit. (That this is only one possibility within the variety of historic understanding and practice is shown by an ancient Eastern tradition which only used oil before baptism but understood this use as a messianic anointing.) The long Christian tradition of prayer and the use of oil points to the appropriateness of such practices as part of Christian baptism. It also points to the dangers of over-systematizing the relationship of such prayer and action to God's activity in the whole process of baptism. Neat attempts to apportion grace to particular parts of the rite fall foul of history as well as theology. This complex tradition raises questions about the common practice of regarding the Orthodox post-baptismal anointing called 'chrismation' as a simple equivalent to the Western practice of confirmation.[8]

---

[8] *The Western Church, and to this day the Church of England, uses the term confirmation in different and often overlapping senses. It has been applied to different parts of the process of incorporation into Christ:*

- *To establish or secure. This is the earliest and non-technical sense. It is used of an action in which the Church accepts and acts on baptism. It was applied to the first receiving of communion as well as to episcopal anointing and hand-laying.*
- *A post-baptismal episcopal rite. In the ninth century this technical sense attaches itself to the exclusively Western practice of a post-baptismal episcopal rite. There has been a continuing debate in the West as to whether this 'confirmation' consists of the general prayer for the sevenfold gift of the Spirit said over all the candidates or of the specific act of praying for each candidate that follows the general prayer.*

At the present time the Church of England is involved in a measure of review about the best structures to support those who are coming to faith in Christ and about how to develop, and perhaps adapt, the Western tradition of confirmation. It is clear that the Church of England wishes to retain a role for the bishop in Christian initiation. Against this background the following provision is made in these rites:

- prayers for the candidates are provided at various points during the process of initiation

- provision is made for the use of oil at various points where this is agreed.

The rites recognize, but do not require, the widespread practice of episcopal consecration of oil for anointing the sick, of oil for candidates preparing for baptism, and also of fragrant oil (chrism) to accompany prayer that people may enjoy the blessings and character of the messianic kingdom. The view has been taken that it is consistent with the Western tradition not to limit the use of chrism to confirmation. The use of chrism is therefore also allowed in these rites after baptism, at affirmation of baptismal faith and at reception. This does not imply either that these are confirmation in the sense in which the law and formularies of the Church of England use this term, or that the use of oil is essential to confirmation. The use of oil may allow those involved to enter into a wealth of biblical imagery about the blessings of the messianic salvation. Simplicity and symbolic coherence require that fragrant oil should only be applied once to an individual candidate in a particular service.

Particular features of the service

1 The sign of the cross

The baptism service has not followed the ASB in allowing the giving of the sign of the cross at one of two places but has placed this firmly at the end of the Decision. Having two positions sends out confusing signals about the function of this action. It often led to the inappropriate use of the prayer for deliverance after baptism and contributed to the occasional abuse of making the sign of the cross in water and regarding that as the baptism. The Prayer Book position, reflecting Cranmer's experience, arose in a situation when infant baptism was universal and the unquestioned norm, and where the medieval rites included a number of separate signings. Few churches of

- **To strengthen.** *This understanding of the episcopal rite became widespread in the thirteenth century, having been applied earlier to an adult's need of strength to witness and to resist temptation, and then transferred to children as they approach adulthood.*

- **To approve or recognize.** *In Cranmer's rites the bishop's action is seen as signifying the Church's recognition of the personal faith nurtured in the catechetical process.*

- **To ratify.** *The meaning of individual or personal ratification emerges in the preface added to the confirmation service in the* Book of Common Prayer *(1662).*

The report On the Way *(Section 7.3, pp. 105-6) identifies five concerns or aspects of Christian life which in Anglicanism have come to be focused on confirmation. The report also notes that: 'In an episcopally ordered Church the bishop is the chief minister of the whole process of Christian initiation and is integral to its practice' (7.5).*

Reformation inheritance adopted the custom of a post-baptismal signing. The pre-baptismal position for the signing fits well with the catechumenal approach to baptism and allows the Decision to be seen as the climax of a period of spiritual preparation, where the sign of the cross is a badge of Christian discipleship embraced after the Decision and before the waters of death and resurrection.

2 Prayer over the Water

Within the service the main theological statement about baptism is made in the baptismal Prayer over the Water. The provision of seasonal baptismal prayers reflects the recommendation of *On The Way* that Church of England baptism services should recognize times other than Easter as appropriate for baptism. These prayers represent a conscious broadening of baptismal imagery beyond the narrowly Paschal. Although there is a strong Western tradition of Paschal emphasis, older Western rites retained a broader and more complex range of images.

Opinions differ about the usefulness of congregational responses or refrains with these prayers; in certain circumstances their use, said or sung, can help carry forward what some experience as a lengthy text. Responsive versions of the baptismal prayer can be found in Appendix 3.

3 The baptism

The traditional Anglican rubrical preference for administration of baptism by dipping (the root meaning of the Greek *baptizo*) has been preserved. In the light of questions raised in certain ecumenical discussions about the validity of Anglican baptisms where the candidates are merely dabbed with water, the following sentence was added to Note 12 of the baptism service: 'The use of a substantial amount of water is desirable; water must at least flow on the skin of the candidate.'

4 Clothing

The explicit provision for clothing after baptism was prompted by three concerns:

- .the practical necessity for some form of clothing to take place immediately after the increasing number of baptisms involving immersion (or submersion). There is scope for making something positive out of a practical necessity

- there are some places with lively family traditions of the christening gown. There is an opportunity to build on existing popular custom, particularly where infants are clothed after the water baptism

- accompanying clothing with text points up a vivid acting out of biblical language about 'putting on' Christ.

Any text should be seen primarily as an accompaniment to the action. Use of this optional provision allows the momentum of the service to be sustained in a context where the need for drying and clothing can easily give rise to a hiatus. Although in many parochial contexts the need for clothing is still hardly experienced (being more frequently required in the case of adult candidates), its inclusion in the rite gives a clear signal that, on the occasions when some form of clothing is a necessity, there is opportunity to highlight its theological significance.

5 Prayers of Intercession

A short form of the Prayers of Intercession or Prayers of the People is included in the baptism service to be used before or after the Welcome and Peace. The rationale for this inclusion is that one of the responsibilities of the newly baptized within the Church is to take their proper place, as members of the royal priesthood, in the privilege and responsibility of public intercession. There is also a danger that without such provision the service may fail to acknowledge the responsibility that all Christians have to share in God's mission to the world.

6 The candle

The optional presentation of a lighted candle to the newly baptized has been placed at the end of the service. The decision to do this was not lightly made and followed experiment in a number of contexts. The text makes a link with the renunciation of darkness, referring back to the lighting of a candle at the Decision. More importantly, it indicates that the primary symbolism is a summons to shine in the world, which is appropriate to the Sending Out of the whole people of God.

Approaching the Baptism of Adults

Increasingly people are coming to baptism as adults. *On The Way*, following the 1991 International Anglican Consultation at Toronto, proposes that such baptisms should be supported by what it calls a catechumenal process in which baptism is integrated within the journey to faith:

> The catechumenal process begins with the welcome of individuals, the valuing of their story, the recognition of the work of God in their lives, the provision of sponsors to accompany their journey, and the engagement of the whole Christian community in both supporting them and learning from them. It seeks to promote personal formation of the new believer in four areas: formation in the Christian tradition as made available in the scriptures, development in personal prayer, incorporation in the worship of the church, and ministry in society, particularly to the powerless, the sick, and all in need...

The Liturgical Commission is currently preparing public forms of prayer to support someone who chooses to be known as an enquirer exploring the Christian faith. They are also preparing forms of prayer to support adults who are preparing for baptism or to renew their baptism in confirmation or an affirmation of baptismal faith.

When adults are baptized the rules of the Church of England allow them to be admitted to communion when they are 'confirmed or ready and desirous to be confirmed'. This allows two practices. In the first the adult is baptized and confirmed by the bishop in the one service and so admitted to communion (at this or a subsequent service). In the second the adult is baptized in the parish and subsequently brought to the bishop for confirmation. He or she may be admitted to communion at their baptism or after the confirmation.

Approaching the Baptism of Children

Baptism, like birth, cannot be a painless or quick experience if it is to achieve its intended purpose. Whether the baptism of young children is performed at the main Sunday gathering or in some other context, it requires the active participation of the Church as well as of the parents and godparents. The baptism service is designed to help this whenever baptism takes place. Baptism must be more than a quick transaction performed before a disengaged, or even disapproving, regular congregation.

Why can strong feelings arise over baptism of young children?

On The Way identifies a sharp clash of expectations that can occur when parents with little active church involvement bring their children for baptism:

> One of the main difficulties in implementing any pastoral approach... is the severe clash of expectations that quickly arise between non-churchgoing parents and clergy or congregations. Parents may well be moved by little more than social convention or they may have profound but inarticulate feelings of their child's need of God's favour; they are likely to have very little sense of what may be expected or asked of them. Clergy and congregation are often sharply aware of the demands as well as joys of public Christian discipleship. The two groups have very different starting points and there is often, in the nature of things, too little time for the clash of expectations to be explored. (5.24)

The report suggests three pastoral priorities for handling this clash of expectations:

- encouraging the congregation to see itself as a baptized people committed to mission

- respectful engagement with the starting point of unchurched parents

- the creation of space and an appropriate context in which genuine encounter and welcome can occur. (5.31)

The baptism service is intended to help manage this clash and provides a framework for a continuing relationship with the family. The Liturgical Commission hopes to publish other forms of service to recognize and support families in the journey that surrounds the birth and upbringing of a young child.

Proxy speaking and parental faith

On The Way discusses the question of how parental faith relates to the baptism of children (pp. 84-90). It contrasts the absence of any explicit demand in the *Book of Common Prayer* with the requirement in the ASB that parents and godparents acknowledge that they speak 'for themselves and for these children' in making the baptismal renunciations and profession of faith. It identifies two issues of substance.

The first is the legitimacy of the bracketing together of the parents' and infant's baptismal profession. This risks disguising the real commitment to Christ being made on behalf of the child in the act of baptism, a matter which stands out clearly in the *Book of Common Prayer* and the tradition which precedes it, and which is focused in the ancient practice of proxy vows. There is also an objection to requiring that parents should make a personal commitment of the seriousness of a baptismal commitment at the moment when the child, and not themselves, is the focus of the service.

Secondly the report discusses whether such a requirement is to be defended on pastoral or on theological grounds. (Some have appeared to argue that only the children of believers are within God's covenant of grace.) Noting the strong New Testament insistence that membership of the people of God is not a matter of blood or racial descent and the fact that 'household' baptism appears to have included slaves and clients as well as blood relatives, it concludes that such a requirement has to be defended on pastoral grounds. It must rest on the pastoral judgement that, in this social context, the child's only chance of the meaningful Christian nurture implied by its baptism is the full involvement of a believing parent. The report noted as a basic problem with this pastoral defence that it does not take seriously the starting point of many parents, and therefore risks asking too much too soon and forcing people to make statements in the service for which they are not yet ready.

The Liturgical Commission framed its original proposals with these considerations in mind and the matter was discussed at length by the Revision Committee at two stages in the Synodical revision of the service. At an early stage the Revision Committee identified that there was an equal division of views among its members on some of the underlying issues raised by these rites and recognized that its task was to provide one service acceptable to, and able to be used by, all shades of opinion in the Church. In the event the Revision Committee accepted that the service should deal with questions to parents and godparents separately from the candidate's baptismal renunciation, and return to the classic form of a proxy decision spoken in the name of an infant candidate. There was unanimous agreement about the wording of the two questions to parents and godparents at the Presentation of the Candidates.

In framing the questions to parents and godparents, the Revision Committee was agreed that a committed Christian faith is presupposed in parents and godparents, but that in practice the extent of such faith is often limited and unarticulated. Equally, whatever text is required of parents must be spoken with integrity and without suspicion of hypocrisy; questions ought not to ask more than can realistically be expected. The rationale for the texts offered is that the godparental role begins at baptism and continues with the child's subsequent journey of faith. That journey is to be accomplished in the life and worship of the Church and this needs to be articulated. The rationale of the order of events in the rite now presented is that:

- there is one service of baptism for all candidates, of whatever age

- at the Presentation of the Candidates parent(s) and sponsors must clearly express a willingness to seek baptism on behalf of candidates unable to answer for themselves and to support them in their journey of faith, including helping them take their place in the worshipping community

- the service should recognize that the parent(s)' primary concern is with their child and should recognize that parents' and godparents' own journey of faith should develop alongside that of child candidates within the life of the Church. While a high level of serious commitment to the child's development is required of parents and godparents of child candidates, this needs to be expressed in terms of encouragement and to recognize that baptismal sponsors are themselves still on a journey of faith which they will continue in companionship with the newly baptized

- the decisions and affirmation of faith are made in the name of the candidates

- after the baptism itself the implications for those supporting them in the journey of faith are appropriately spelt out

- it is, of course, presupposed that pastoral practice secures an explanation of this rationale to the parents, godparents and sponsors in advance of the service itself.

How does the service involve the congregation?

The service involves the congregation in actively welcoming a child who comes to baptism along with his/her parents and godparents, in professing the Christian faith into which the child is baptized, in praying for child and parents in their life together, and in charging them to join them in a common witness to Christ in the world.

How does the service involve the parents and godparents?

In welcoming the parents and godparents, the service is careful to recognize that their primary motivation is concern for the child and his/her future welfare. The parents and godparents may present a child for baptism; they ask for God's help in walking with their child 'in the way of Christ'; they may sign the child with the sign of the cross after the Decision, and may dress the child in a christening gown after baptism; they are prayed for by the whole congregation after the short charge at the Commission, and may receive a lighted candle on the child's behalf.

Confirmation

The practice of confirmation in the Church of England is governed by Canon B 27 and the authorized liturgical texts, and conforms carefully to a tradition that has evolved in the Western church. The high pastoral profile of confirmation within the mission of the Church was largely a development of the nineteenth century and there is continuing debate about its precise relation to admission to communion and to the development of mature faith in those baptized in infancy. Some of these debates are summarized in *On The Way* (pp. 63-9,104-6) and are closely related to questions of the role of the bishop in Christian initiation (cf *On The Way* pp. 106-9). (See also footnote 8 on page 195.)

The confirmation services authorized in this provision follow carefully traditional Anglican practice and make no attempt to resolve these difficult questions. On all views confirmation derives its meaning from baptism. The structure of the confirmation services therefore conforms carefully to the baptism service and has a similar inherent logic and flow.

The tradition that confirmation is unrepeatable and normally administered in adolescence to those baptized in infancy has meant that significant moments and crises in people's subsequent growth in faith go unmarked in the public life of the Church. Other Anglican Provinces, and also the British Joint Liturgical Group, have made liturgical provision for some of these moments. These are reflected in new provision for a public Affirmation of Baptismal Faith and for the Reception into the Communion of the Church of England.

Affirmation of Baptismal Faith

Many people make an important step of personal commitment after they have been baptized and confirmed, and feel the need for God's grace to be acknowledged before the Church. The form prescribed gives opportunity for this to take place in public worship and relates the person's new commitment to the grace of God pledged to them in their past baptism. This form may be used at a service led by the bishop (pp. 103-17) or as part of the ordinary worship of a parish (pp. 162-73).

Explicit provision for a personal affirmation of baptismal faith follows requests from the House of Bishops and the General Synod for more vivid recognition of post-baptismal experiences of personal renewal and commitment. The provision here draws on examples found elsewhere in the Anglican Communion as well as in significant ecumenical material. The possibility of candidates signing themselves with water from the font or being sprinkled with water by the bishop or president picks up practices common in some sections of the Church and enables a stronger ritual sign to be used without giving any appearance of a second baptism.

Reception into the Communion of the Church of England

Canon B 28 governs the reception of people into the communion of the Church of England. The interpretation of the requirement for episcopal confirmation has become more complex in the light of the increased use of presbyteral confirmation (with chrism) in the Roman Catholic Church, the regular practice of presbyteral confirmation (without chrism) in the Nordic Churches of the Porvoo Agreement, and continuing debate about how presbyteral chrismation is to be understood in the Eastern churches. The provision made in these services makes no attempt to resolve such questions. It is provided to enable the public reception into the communicant life of the Church of England of those who are judged to be episcopally confirmed.

The question of whether this should be celebrated publicly before the bishop or more quietly will depend on individual circumstances. Where an episcopally ordained priest is being received, the Canons require that this must be done before the bishop. The current discipline of the Church of England requires that members of the Church of England who have not been episcopally confirmed must be confirmed before they can be regarded as full communicant members of the Church of England. Members of other Churches who have not been episcopally confirmed in the sense intended under Canon B 15A become communicant members of the Church of England by being confirmed by an Anglican bishop. While this discipline stands, reception into the communion of the Church of England is for those who have been episcopally confirmed in other churches.

Frequently Asked Questions

What is the difference between a godparent and a sponsor?

The Canons of the Church of England (Canon B 23) recognize both sponsors, who support candidates for baptism, and godparents, who take on their role at the baptism of children. The baptism service recognizes both a social and a spiritual role for godparents in the lives of their godchildren. The minister can dispense godparents from the normal requirement that a godparent should be confirmed. It is possible for a child to have additional sponsors as well as godparents who also agree to support them in their continuing journey to a mature faith.

Why is there seasonal provision?

The ancient church of the West has traditionally associated baptism with Easter. However, other traditions in the Church have associated baptism with other times in the church year, particularly the Epiphany and the Baptism of Christ. There are practical difficulties with trying to hold all baptisms at Easter. These services therefore provide for baptisms at any time

– General – as well as around Easter, Epiphany and All Saints' tide. Appendix 3 includes responsive forms of the Prayer over the Water; these can be used to involve the congregation, particularly by the use of a cantor and appropriate congregational music.

When may oil be used?

The use of oil is allowed for in the Notes and an explanation of the background and meaning of this practice, taken from the First Report of the Revision Committee, can be found on pages 194-6.

Olive oil may be used to sign candidates with the cross after the Decision. The fragrant oil called chrism may be used after the baptism with the prayer on page 26 but, in any case, must not be used more than once for the same person in a service. The view has been taken that chrism may be used more than once in a person's journey of faith.

Can families be baptized together?

Yes. This is provided for in Note 8 on page 17 and Note 1 on page 99. It will probably be appropriate to use the short address from the Commission for children able to understand for themselves.

When can the shorter form of Affirmation of Faith (Appendix 7) be used?

The rubric on page 25 limits the use of this form to 'strong pastoral reasons' out of a desire to honour the Anglican commitment (embodied in the 1888 Lambeth Quadrilateral) that the Apostles' Creed be regarded as the 'baptismal symbol', that is, the form of the public baptismal profession to which the Church is committed. The shorter form can be used when the Apostles' Creed is regarded for good reason as being too long or too complicated.

When is it appropriate to use the thanksgiving prayer from Appendix 1?

This is not intended to replace the Thanksgiving and Blessing for a Child which itself is best seen as a preliminary (rather than an alternative) to baptism. However, it is provided for those situations when the baptism service itself needs also to acknowledge the parents' desire to thank God for the birth or adoption of a child.

What should happen when a child or adult is baptized in danger of death and then lives?

The services make provision for a public celebration that completes the welcome into the life of the Church – see page 96. Note 2 to the form for Emergency Baptism (page 94) makes clear that parents 'should be assured that questions of ultimate salvation or of the provision of a Christian funeral for an infant who dies do not depend upon whether or not the child has been baptized'.

What is envisaged by 'testimony'?

This does not necessarily imply one particular style of personal presentation. The intention is that, in some circumstances, individuals may value the opportunity to give a brief personal explanation (out loud or in written form) of how they have come to faith.

Can the Signing with the Cross take place after the Baptism?

The possibility of signing with the cross at the prayer after the Baptism is provided for, but if this is done it should be accompanied by the text provided at that point in the rite, 'May God who has received you ...', not the text provided for the Signing with the Cross after the Decision. If signing takes place after the Baptism, it must follow the administration of water as a separate action. If no signing takes place after the Decision, the words at the foot of page 22 are omitted, together with those at the top of page 23 beginning, 'Do not be ashamed ...' Only the prayer, 'May almighty God deliver you ...' is used to conclude the Decision. None of these words are used after the Baptism.

However, it is possible to make the sign of the cross in both places. If oil of chrism is used at the prayer at the top of page 26, this may also be accompanied by the sign of the cross, or a chi-rho ☧, signifying *Christos*, the Anointed One.

Copyright Information

The Central Board of Finance of the Church of England and the other copyright owners and administrators of texts included in *Initiation Services* have given permission for the use of their material in local reproductions on a non-commercial basis which comply with the conditions for reproductions for local use set out in the Central Board of Finance's booklet, *A Brief Guide to Liturgical Copyright*. This is available from Church House Bookshop, Great Smith Street, London SW1P 3BN (Tel: 0171-340-0276/0277; Fax: 0171-340-0278/0281; e-mail: info@chp.u-net.com) or from other Christian bookshops. A reproduction which meets the conditions stated in that booklet may be made without an application for copyright permission or payment of a fee, but the following copyright acknowledgement must be included:

Common Worship: Initiation Services, material from which is included in this service, is copyright © The Central Board of Finance of the Church of England, 1997, 1998.

Permission must be obtained in advance for any reproduction which does not comply with the conditions set out in *A Brief Guide to Liturgical Copyright*. Applications for permission should be addressed to: The Copyright Manager, Central Board of Finance, Church House, Great Smith Street, London SW1P 3NZ (Tel: 0171-340-0275; Fax: 0171-340-0281).

Acknowledgements and Sources

The publisher gratefully acknowledges permission to reproduce copyright material in this book. Every effort has been made to trace and contact copyright holders. If there are any inadvertent omissions we apologize to those concerned and undertake to include suitable acknowledgements in all future editions.

Published sources include the following:

The Central Board of Finance of the Church of England: *The Alternative Service Book 1980*; *The Promise of His Glory*, 1991; new work by the Liturgical Commission of the General Synod of the Church of England and material produced by the General Synod and its House of Bishops, all of which are copyright © The Central Board of Finance of the Church of England.

General Synod of the Anglican Church of Canada: Based on (or excerpted from) *The Book of Alternative Services of the Anglican Church of Canada*, copyright © 1985. Used with permission:

'We thank you, Almighty God, for the gift of water' (pp. 23-4)

'Will you continue in the apostles' teaching and fellowship' (p. 28)

English Language Liturgical Consultation: The text of the Apostles' Creed (pp. 24-5) from *Praying Together* (Canterbury Press Norwich, 1988) is copyright © the English Language Liturgical Consultation 1988.

Episcopal Church of the USA: *The Book of Common Prayer* according to the use of the Episcopal Church of the USA, 1979 on which no copyright is claimed.

'Blessed be God, Father, Son and Holy Spirit' (p. 103)

The Joint Liturgical Group of Great Britain: Collects and prayers from *The Daily Office Revised*. Copyright © the Joint Liturgical Group of Great Britain and reproduced by permission:

'God of mercy and love, in baptism you welcome the sinner (p. 112, adapted)

'God of mercy and love, by one Spirit we have all been baptized into one body' (pp. 112-13, adapted)

The European Province of the Society of St Francis: *Celebrating Common Prayer: A version of The Daily Office SSF*, 1992. Copyright © The Society of St Francis and extracts reproduced by permission:

'As a royal priesthood, let us pray to the Father' (pp. 28-9, adapted)

The Right Reverend David Stancliffe, Bishop of Salisbury: copyright © David S. Stancliffe. Reproduced by permission:

'And now we give you thanks ... and renew us in the image of your glory' (p. 30)

'God, who in his Christ gives us a spring of water ... image of his glory' (p. 76)

'Lord, in the vision of your heavenly kingdom ... one God, for ever and ever' (p. 83; adapted from the Society of St Francis, *Celebrating Common Prayer*, p. 600, Psalm Collect No. 87)

'God has called you by name and made you his own' (p. 112)